THE COMMON CORE STATE STANDARDS IN LITERACY SERIES

A series designed to help educators successfully
implement CCSS literacy standards in K–12 classrooms

SUSAN B. NEUMAN AND D. RAY REUTZEL, EDITORS
SERIES BOARD: Diane August, Linda Gambrell, Steve Graham, Laura Justice,
Margaret McKeown, and Timothy Shanahan

T0369718

The **Fluency Factor**

Authentic Instruction and Assessment for Reading Success in the Common Core Classroom

**Timothy Rasinski and
James K. Nageldinger**

Foreword by Patricia M. Cunningham

TEACHERS COLLEGE PRESS

TEACHERS COLLEGE | COLUMBIA UNIVERSITY
NEW YORK AND LONDON

Published by Teachers College Press, 1234 Amsterdam Avenue, New York, NY 10027

Library of Congress Cataloging-in-Publication Data is available at loc.gov

Names: Rasinski, Timothy V., author. I Nageldinger, James K.
Title: The fluency factor : authentic assessment and instruction for reading
    success in the common core classroom / Timothy Rasinski, James K.
    Nageldinger.
Description: New York : Teachers College Press, Teachers College, Columbia
    University, 2016. I Series: The common core state standards in literacy series
    I Includes bibliographical references and index.
Identifiers: LCCN 2015034033I ISBN 9780807757475 (pbk. : alk. paper) I ISBN
    9780807774540 (ebook)
Subjects: LCSH: Reading comprehension—Study and teaching (Elementary) I
    Reading (Elementary)—United States. I Reading (Elementary)—Standards—
    United States.
Classification: LCC LB1573.7 .R34 2016 I DDC 372.47--dc23
LC record available at http://lccn.loc.gov/2015034033
ISBN 978-0-8077-5747-5 (paper)
ISBN 978-0-8077-7454-0 (ebook)

Printed on acid-free paper
Manufactured in the United States of America

Contents

Foreword

I hate to admit it, but I agreed to write this foreword only because Tim and I have been lifelong friends and I have so much respect for what he has done for struggling readers. The reason I didn't want to write this foreword is because the book is about fluency and I, like the teachers referred to in the introduction, had become disenchanted with the whole notion of fluency.

At Wake Forest, we have a small elementary education program and each spring I teach my juniors their literacy course. In the fall, I follow them into the field as they do their student teaching. Walking down the halls, I see numerous adults sitting and "clocking" children as they read aloud. At the end of one minute, the tester stops the child and plots the number of words correctly read to the child's graph. The child is either congratulated for "reading faster this week than last week" or encouraged to "practice reading fast" so that the graph can show a jump in reading speed next week.

"This is a travesty," I think. "How can we have created an assessment system that makes our children think that reading faster is the goal? " I blame the National Reading Panel and Reading First for their insistence on regular "progress monitoring," which has led to this simplistic and pervasive testing.

In the spring of their senior year, I teach my seniors a course in which they tutor struggling readers who are in 4th or 5th grade. We use graded passages and word lists to determine whether word identification, language comprehension, or reading comprehension is their area of greatest need. For most of these struggling readers, their word identification levels and listening comprehension levels are higher than their silent reading comprehension levels. They have the decoding and word recognition skills to read text at a higher level than the text they can comprehend, and they can comprehend text at a higher level when it is read to them. Why then do they have lower levels of comprehension when they read silently?

Jessica, for example, is a 5th-grader who cannot read silently. When reminded to read it "to herself," she mouths each word as she reads it. Carl reads silently but finishes a short passage in no time at all and comprehends very little. When asked to read the same passage aloud, he reads as fast as he can, skipping any word he does not immediately recognize. Paul reads in a monotone, pronouncing each word carefully and paying no attention to punctuation. If you closed your eyes and just listened to him, you would think you were listening to him read a list of words.

If fluent, expressive reading is the bridge between word identification and comprehension, all these children have not found that bridge. They are saying the words as quickly and accurately as they can and are convinced that is what you are supposed to do when you read. It is not surprising that older children who were subjected to weekly one-minute oral reading speed testing would learn to do what they were being measured on.

So, I began to read *The Fluency Factor* reluctantly, determined to find something positive to say in my foreword! Well, imagine how delighted I was to find that the authors had taken on the speed, assessment, and boring repeated readings practices head-on and presented wonderfully doable assessments and classroom activities that would truly teach children to read fluently and develop expressive reading as the bridge between word identification and comprehension.

Tim and James state that "if fluency involves reading with expression, then there are authentic and engaging reading experiences (and texts) that lend themselves to expressive reading performances." They then devote most of the page space in this book to activities you can use to make "authentic fluency instruction . . . the most important and engaging 20–30 minutes of the school day."

Most of us get discouraged and "give up" when something we have worked so hard on gets distorted and misused. Tim has been an advocate for fluency for as long as I have known him. I am delighted that he didn't just let it go and that this new book might just spark a resurrection of "authentic fluency instruction."

—Patricia M. Cunningham, Wake Forest University

The **Fluency Factor**

CHAPTER 1

Haven't You Heard?
Fluency Is NOT Hot!

We recently had a chance to visit a school in a nearby city, where we had previously spoken to teachers and administrators about reading fluency. We were interested in seeing how their thoughts about and approaches to teaching reading fluency have evolved since our last visit a few years earlier. We were struck by the comments of several teachers—one teacher said to us, "Oh, we don't do fluency anymore; I want my 1st-graders to focus on comprehension, not reading fast." A 3rd-grade teacher said, "I've decided to integrate my fluency instruction into silent reading time. As my students read silently, I prompt them to be sure to read quickly and expressively." Over half the teachers we visited in this school had developed either a negative view of reading fluency or had decided that it could be left to a comment or two made prior to students' silent reading.

This is not an uncommon finding in schools across the country. Reading fluency's place in the school reading curriculum has diminished significantly. And it's not just how teachers approach reading fluency. Even scholars of reading seem to have developed a negative view of reading fluency. For the past several years, the International Literacy Association has sponsored an annual survey of scholars' opinions of literacy topics that are hot and not hot. Topics such as comprehension and standards have been consistently rated as hot. However, from 2008 through 2014 the scholars in the survey have identified reading fluency as a "not hot" topic. Moreover, the scholars were also of the opinion that fluency "should not be hot."

Now, we can argue about what "hot" and "not hot" means in the context of this survey. Is it that these scholars feel fluency is not an important competency worth pursuing instructionally? Or is it that although fluency may be an important competency, the way it is actually approached in instructional settings leaves much to be desired?

Or is it that fluency is simply not on the current cutting edge of topics on which some scholars are focused? Regardless of which rationale has made fluency "not hot" for half a decade, the source of concern remains that it, fluency, is not generally viewed in a positive light by those—reading teachers and scholars—in the know.

If fluency is not hot, then some teachers might wonder why we are writing a book about it. Certainly, who would want to read a book on a topic that is not considered valuable for student growth and improvement? Yet, even though some teachers do not believe fluency has value in the classroom, we believe that reading fluency is indeed important. In fact, we feel that learning to read fluently is critical for student success. Because many students fail to achieve sufficient levels of fluency for their age or grade level, this, in turn, can lead to difficulties in other reading areas such as comprehension, motivation for reading, and self-confidence.

The problem with fluency's lack of heat, as we see it, is the way that many well-meaning and dedicated reading teachers have defined and approached it instructionally. Early definitions of reading fluency almost always include some reference to speed of reading (e.g., National Reading Panel, 2000). Indeed, one of the easiest ways some teachers choose to measure reading fluency is to have students read a grade-level text for 1 minute and then count the number of words they were able to read correctly. Research has shown that this measure of reading fluency correlates remarkably well with reading comprehension and other measures of general reading competency. And so, because some teachers define and connect fluency through this measure, a number of publishers developed several reading fluency programs for teaching reading fluency that intentionally or unintentionally communicate to teachers and students that the goal of reading fluency is to foster faster reading. Because teachers continue to focus on fluency and speed, some students are able to read quickly but are unable to comprehend/understand what they've read. They blow through punctuation, minimize pausing and reflection, read in a monotone, and end their reading without good comprehension or much satisfaction.

No wonder fluency is not hot. If this is what defines fluency, we would certainly share these students and teachers' sentiments.

We think that speed, one aspect of fluency, is one good way of tracking students' growth in this area. However, we don't feel that simply teaching students to read more quickly is the way to improve their fluency. Speed in reading is a consequence, not a cause, of fluency. We do want students to become faster readers, but we want them to become fast in the same ways that all of you reading this book became reasonably fast readers. Do you recall how you became a fast reader? Did someone judge you based solely on how quickly you read? Were you in a reading program that focused solely on speed? Did you have a teacher who encouraged you regularly to read faster each day? We think not.

We think you became a fast reader the same way we became fast readers—by reading frequently, orally, and silently. We read by ourselves, with parents, teachers, and classmates, and in various groups. As we read, we learned to recognize words more effortlessly and efficiently and, as a result, our speed increased. With increased efficiency in word recognition, we were more able to move our cognitive resources away from word recognition to the more important task of comprehension. So speed and comprehension improved through practice in reading.

Fluency's relative demise has also been because of its predominant association with oral reading. We talk about fluent oral speakers; it follows that fluency in reading is also associated with oral language production. After all, we can only observe fluency in reading during oral reading. So, the thinking goes, because fluency is about oral reading and most of the reading done by adults is silent reading, why should fluency matter for most readers? The truth of the matter is that the way one reads orally reflects how one reads silently. It is likely that when coming across a difficult word to decode or sound out, a reader will be challenged, whether reading it orally or silently. So we take that position that fluency may be observed orally, but it still happens when reading silently. In fact, eye movement in reading research (Samuels, Rasinski, & Hiebert, 2011) suggests that fluency is a major factor for proficient silent reading.

Fluency has also been dismissed by some because it is a competency associated with the early stages of literacy development. Some models of reading development view it as something to be achieved in the primary grades (Chall, 1996). Again, though we see that fluency is indeed a competency that we want students to develop as early in their school careers as possible, the Common Core State Standards call fluency a "foundational" reading skill, a competency upon which other, more sophisticated competencies, developed later in a student's school career, rely (National Governors Association Center for Best Practices & Council of Chief State School Officers, 2010).

The problem with thinking of fluency only as a primary grade competency is that fluency is, in a sense, a relative concept; that is, a reader's fluency or lack of fluency is relative to the difficulty of the

THINK ABOUT IT

What memories do you have of your own learning to read in school? Jot down the memories, both positive and negative, that you can recall. Which ones were most positive and why? Which tended to be negative? Were there any things that your teachers did that improved your ability to read fluently (with automatic word recognition and appropriate expression in oral reading)? Do you recall events that may have affected your fluency in a negative way? What can we do to make the positive aspects of your learning to read fluency a regular and integral part of your own instruction?

WHAT WE THINK

We think that people have a tendency to repeat what has occurred in the past. Much of the way all of us learned to read is probably a good way for many children to learn to read. The problem is that we often repeat the negative as well as the positive experiences we have had. The key is to sort out the negative from the positive and intentionally try to maximize the positive aspects of fluency instruction, while minimizing the negative.

Tim (one of the authors of this book) recalls having to read orally in class during round-robin reading. On most occasions, he was able to read with decent fluency. But because he seldom had a chance to preview the readings before the teacher called on him, he would sometimes stumble on several words and had to have the teacher call on him to "sound out" each difficult word. These practices did not seem to improve Tim's reading. Rather, they contributed to a decrease in self-confidence as a reader, an increase in shame for reading poorly, and an increase in embarrassment for subjecting his classmates to listening to a rendering of a text that was far from fluent or meaningful.

text the reader is reading. A student may read a 3rd-grade passage fluently, but the same student might not read a text written at a 5th-grade level fluently. Our point here is that, yes, fluency is something that students should master early on with grade-level texts. However, as students graduate to more challenging texts, the fluent reading of these texts must evolve as well. Even as adults we sometimes encounter texts that would challenge our fluency (Tim has been working with a lawyer on developing a will. The documents that the attorney has been sending to Tim have caused considerable disfluency—and frustration—in his reading fluency and comprehension.)

If teachers do not continually develop fluency in their students, some students will fall behind in their reading fluency relative to the texts they are asked to read. Several studies have demonstrated a strong correlation between various measures of reading fluency and more-general measures of reading achievement, including comprehension in the middle and secondary grades (Paige, Rasinski, & Magpuri-Lavell, 2012; Rasinski, Padak, McKeon, Krug-Wilfong, Friedauer, & Heim, 2005; Rasinski, Riki, & Johnston, 2009). Moreover, the same studies have found that a significant number of students who struggle in their overall reading achievement are well below what we might consider minimal levels of proficiency in their fluency. So, if you happen to be a teacher in the middle or secondary grades, this book is for you, too!

THINK ABOUT IT

Do you have students who you think struggle with fluency? What behaviors do they exhibit that lead you to this observation? What do you see as the consequences to these students' fluency problems? Does it affect their reading in other ways? Does it have an impact on how they feel about reading? How does it affect how they feel about themselves as readers? Do you see any connection between problems in fluency and students' reading and learning in other subject areas? What other observations do you have?

WHAT WE THINK

You probably can predict what we think about students who struggle in reading fluency. Granted, they struggle in other areas of reading across the curriculum. But perhaps the greatest impediment we see is in students' attitudes toward reading; they dislike it because they lack confidence in themselves as readers. Students who struggle in reading often publicly demonstrate their lack of proficiency in fluency, as compared perhaps to more fluent peers, because they doubt their own ability to become proficient readers. This lack of confidence then causes them to avoid reading, because reading does not bring them much satisfaction. And this leads to more relative regression in fluency, a growing lack of confidence, and even less reading.

WHY THIS BOOK ON FLUENCY?

This brief exploration of reading fluency captures the genesis of this book. It's not so much that fluency should not be hot; rather, we think it is the methods that have been developed, mandated, and implemented for instruction in and measurement of fluency that have caused it to be not hot. If teachers could revisit how they measure and approach reading fluency, it could shift back to a hot topic for students and teachers again.

Our goal in writing this book is to share with you our ideas about reading fluency. The information we will share with you comes from many scholars and teachers who have thought about, conducted research on, and developed and implemented effective instruction on reading fluency. In writing this book, we hope that readers may get a different view of reading fluency. Essentially, we hope to convince you that we need to take another look at how reading fluency may be approached instructionally. The "read for speed" approach just does not cut it anymore; students and teachers need alternative strategies to make fluency hot once again.

SOME NEW THINKING ABOUT FLUENCY

This book provides you with a framework for thinking about reading fluency as a critical factor for proficient reading. In the first chapter, we hope to get our readers to put aside some of those bandwagon notions about reading fluency—that it's about reading fast, that it's only for younger readers, and that it is only about oral reading. There is so much more to fluency.

Chapter 2 begins with a brief historical overview of fluency. Although fluency seemed to gain traction in the reading field after the publication of the report of the National Reading Panel (2000), it has been around for much longer. In fact, some of the earliest goals in reading instruction in the United States were fluency related. Fluency is not a unitary competency; there are multiple dimensions to fluency beyond just having children read quickly and expressively. It is about helping readers make meaning as they read. Many readers struggle with reading comprehension because they have not achieved sufficient levels of fluency in their reading.

Most books that discuss reading instruction begin, after a short introduction, with information on the most effective instruction, and assessment is generally discussed later in the text. After learning about the nature of reading fluency, we feel it is more appropriate to first learn about assessing or measuring students' level of fluency on the various components of fluency. This provides readers with tools they can use immediately to determine whether their own students are making adequate progress and/or improving in response to certain instructional fluency methods. Much in the same way that before learning to drive a car one should first learn about the tools available in the automobile for measuring speed and other important factors related to driving, the ability to measure fluency and progress in fluency, we feel, sets the stage for learning how to improve reading fluency.

Many books on instruction put assessment at the end of the book. We feel that understanding the nature of reading fluency provides teachers with a good sense of how it should be assessed. To that end, we have put assessment of reading fluency in Chapter 3, closer to the book's beginning.

In Chapter 4, we present the essential methods for teaching reading fluency. These methods have been shown to be effective through published research studies as well as through actual classroom practice from our and other teachers' classrooms. Many readers will find that they are familiar with many of the methods, as they have been part and parcel of reading instruction for years. The difference is that these methods can be used intentionally for teaching reading fluency.

In Chapter 5, we offer solutions to the evolving trend of looking at reading scientifically, rather than artistically. The concern we have with the way these methods have been adapted for many of these programs is that they take what we call a scientific approach to fluency. Teachers deliver their instructional methods in a highly structured and sequential way, so their students' fluency is regularly measured using reading speed as the metric. This often results in students reading texts that are quite limited in scope and genre. As a result, many students (and teachers) view reading fluency in a very mechanical manner, where the goal is to improve reading speed through repeated practice of an informational text that does not have an authentic purpose and for no other purpose than to read it fast. We feel that all reading instruction should be treated as an art as well as a science (Rasinski, 2011). In this chapter, we explore ways that you can make fluency instruction more of an artful experience. If fluency involves reading with expression, then there are authentic and engaging reading experiences (and texts) that lend themselves to expressive reading performances.

Chapters 4 and 5 focus on fluency instruction that is appropriate for all students. Unfortunately, despite excellent instruction, some students continue to struggle in becoming fluent readers, and in doing so, they restrict their development in reading comprehension. In Chapter 6, we explore how to help these students who need a more intensive, yet still authentic and engaging, approach to fluency development. For example, we describe a Fluency Development Lesson that we have used in our own reading clinic for over a decade. Regular use of this lesson has led to remarkable gains in fluency and overall reading achievement for most of our students.

In addition to offering classroom-centered strategies to improve fluency, we also offer other suggestions to improve fluency outside of school. Fluency doesn't have to begin at school. Home involvement is critical to students' overall progress in reading; it can also add significantly to students' reading fluency development. The focus for Chapter 7 is how teachers and school administrators can involve parents and other family members in simple yet incredibly effective ways, to promote and develop their children's reading fluency. For example, parents can begin with simple methods, such as reading to their children, reading with their children, and listening to their children read. We conclude the chapter by sharing an instructional approach, adapted from the Fluency Development Lesson for home use, which integrates those methods into a powerful instructional experience.

The final chapter of our book attempts to bring it all together. Up to this point we have explored various aspects of reading fluency: providing background, giving definition, exploring methods of instruction and assessment, and involving the home. In Chapter 8, we invite the teacher, parent, or reading coach to consider ways in which he or she can integrate the information from the previous chapters into a reading fluency program that works best for teachers and students. We provide examples of how teachers have made fluency an important and integral part of their own reading (and writing) curriculum. Using these examples as models, we challenge them to create an effective and artful approach to fluency that readers can find engaging and authentic.

As well as offering definitions, strategies, and suggestions throughout the book, we also offer focal points in each chapter for readers to stop and think about alternative fluency practices for students in and outside the classroom. If you are reading this book with colleagues, we hope you might share your thoughts with one another at these important junctures. In addition to points for collaboration, each chapter has text boxes that offer suggestions for further information or resources or teaching and assessment tools that you can duplicate, adapt, or modify for your own instructional purposes. Each chapter ends with thoughtful stopping points in "What We Think;" here, we present some of our own thinking on the topics at hand.

By writing this book, we affirm our conviction that fluency does matter for all readers, that many students continue to struggle with fluency, that this struggle is a major contributor to other reading and learning problems students may have, and that fluency can be taught in ways that are authentic, engaging, effective, and an integral part of the overall reading curriculum. Our greatest hope is that after reading this book and thoughtfully considering the information presented, you will also see that authentic fluency instruction deserves a significant place in your own reading curriculum. It can become the most important and engaging 20–30 minutes of the school day.

We wish you happy and fluent reading!

CHAPTER 2

What Is Fluency and Why Does It Matter?

Inside Mrs. Radovitch's 3rd-grade classroom you will find a wide variety of readers. Most of her students are progressing nicely—when reading orally or silently, their reading seems to require very little effort. It just seems to flow like a river. Moreover, these students have a good comprehension of nearly everything they read, whether it is informational texts or stories. Mrs. R worries very little about these students because "they have mastered the mechanics of reading. Now what they need to do is continue reading daily, for school and for pleasure, and they will progress on their own."

Mrs. Radovitch saves her worries for the seven students in her class whose reading does not seem to flow like a river. Their comprehension is not nearly as good as the other readers'. Jason and Hamad's reading river seems to have a series of dams that regularly stop or impede the flow of their reading. These students still have significant difficulty in decoding words. They seem to struggle through any word that contains more than one syllable. Indeed, in many cases Jason and Hamad are struggling mightily to decode the words they encounter in oral reading without help. Because of the reading challenges these boys face, Jason and Hamad are in an intervention program in which the focus is on phonics or word decoding.

The other five struggling readers in Mrs. R's class are in the same intervention group as Jason and Hamad. Yet Mrs. R wonders if these five students are benefiting from appropriate instruction like Jason and Hamad. Their reading river does not seem to be dammed up nearly as much as Jason and Hamad's. Rather, the reading for these students might best be characterized as a series of ebbs and flows. Word recognition per se does not seem to be the major problem—they are able to accurately decode the words they encounter while reading. However, when they come to difficult words, they have to slow down, and occasionally stop, as they have to work at decoding certain words. Although accurate word recognition does occur, the additional effort required by these students, along with the frequent stops and starts, slows down their reading and causes their oral reading to sound like something other than authentic language production. They do not read with expression—Mrs. R sometimes calls it "robot reading," and she wonders if placement in an intervention program that focuses on word decoding is the appropriate intervention for these students: "They are pretty good at decoding the words in their reading. The problem is they have to work too hard at it."

We feel that Mrs. Radovitch is correct in her analysis of those five readers. They seem to have conquered the basics of word recognition. What they need now is to become so adept or effortless at it that their reading can flow like a river, their reading can sound like or be expressed as real language, and they can make greater meaning out of the texts they read. These students need to become more fluent readers.

FLUENCY HAS BEEN AROUND A LONG TIME

In recent years, fluency got a toehold in the reading curriculum with the publication of the *Report of the National Reading Panel* (2000). In this review of research related to reading acquisition and effective reading instruction, researchers found that fluency in reading is a necessary component for proficient reading, that reading fluency is an appropriate goal for reading instruction, and that several instructional approaches to fluency instruction hold promise.

However, elements of fluency and fluency instruction can be found in some of the earliest examples of formal reading instruction. "Eloquent oral reading" was a goal of early reading instruction. In 1835, Lyman Cobb (as cited in Smith, 1965) noted that the goal of reading instruction was the development of oral reading skills:

> A just delivery consists in a distinct articulation of words pronounced in proper tones, suitably varied to the sense, and the emotions of the mind; with due attention to accent, to emphasis, in its several gradations; to rests or pauses of the voice, in proper places . . . and the whole accompanied with expressive looks, and significant gestures. . . . (pp. 40–41)

The means to achieve such a goal was in the form of oral read-ing recitation that focused on the elocution or sound of the written passage. A typical lesson involved the teacher orally reading a text to students followed by the students rehearsing the text on their own, and then some students orally recited or performed the passage for the teacher and classmates. The teacher judged students' reading by the quality of the oral reading and the students' recall of the content. This approach became so ingrained in the American schools that philoso-pher William James (1892) noted, "The teacher's success or failure in teaching reading is based, so far as the public estimate is concerned, upon the oral reading method" (p. 422). As a result, teachers began to rely regularly on this method to teach reading fluency.

Over time, school-based reading instruction evolved from an em-phasis on oral reading elocution to silent reading comprehension. Indeed, scholars in the late 19th century noted the glaring lack of emphasis on comprehension. Horace Mann (1891, cited in Hoffman & Segel, 1983) argued that over 90% of students engaged in reading instruction "do not understand the meaning for the words they read" (p. 4). Francis Parker (1894) was even more vehement in his condem-nation of oral reading instruction for elocution.

> Many of the grossest errors in teaching reading spring from confounding the two processes of attention and expression. Reading itself is not expres-sion. . . . Reading is a mental process. . . . Oral reading is expression, and comes under the heading of speech. The custom of making oral reading the principal and almost the only means of teaching reading has led to many errors prevalent to-day. (Parker, 1894, cited in Smith, 1965, p. 159)

Echoing these sentiments, the Indianapolis Public Schools Course of Study for 1902 (as cited in Hyatt, 1943) noted that "Reading . . . fundamentally is not oral expression. Rather, reading is making mean-ing or comprehension" (p. 21). Edmund Huey (1908) noted that oral reading had become a practice that was evident only in schools through activities such as oral recitation and round-robin reading. Conversely, in life outside the classroom, people generally read silently for informa-tion or entertainment.

The growing recognition of silent reading comprehension over oral reading elocution and expression eventually led to the diminishment of oral reading in classrooms. Oral reading, however, did find itself manifested in one peculiar way during the 20th century: round-robin reading. Round-robin oral reading was a method for teachers to monitor a group of students' reading—that is, word recognition—as they took turns reading orally. Expression or fluency was not the focus of round-robin reading.

Although *reading fluency* was not a term used often in reading instruction, when it was invoked, it usually referred to expression in oral reading, and expressive oral reading was not thought to be a primary concern when it came to reading instruction.

Beginning in the 1970s, research began, once again, to explore the role of expressive oral reading (Rasinski & Hoffman, 2003). Simply stated, this research found that fluent, smooth, appropriately fast, and expressive oral reading was associated with good oral and silent reading comprehension. In its comprehensive review of research on factors associated with positive reading outcomes, the National Reading Panel endorsed reading fluency as an important and required competency for successful reading instruction. Subsequent programs and initiatives, such as Reading First and the Common Core State Standards (CCSS), have embraced reading fluency as a requisite part of exemplary reading curricula.

JUST WHAT IS READING FLUENCY?

Fluency is a term that can and has been used in a number of different ways related to reading. In its most general sense, fluency is associated with proficient overall silent or oral reading at any grade level. When readers comprehend what they read, they are reading fluently.

Reading fluency actually consists of two separate competencies that lie between word recognition and comprehension. Traditionally, reading has been viewed as consisting of two major competencies— word recognition (the ability to accurately sound out and acquire the meaning of individual words) and comprehension (the ability to access the meaning that the author of the text is attempting to convey through the words). Both of these competencies need to be taught in reading instruction.

Reading fluency has been described by various scholars as a bridge (Pikulski & Chard, 2005) that links word recognition to comprehension (see Figure 1.1), and unless students traverse this bridge, they are often left on an island of words—vainly attempting to decode or understand the words in the text and thus experiencing difficulty in

Figure 1.1. Fluency: The Bridge to Comprehension

gaining the overall meaning of the text. Word recognition automaticity is half of the fluency bridge. It refers to students' ability to read the words in a text accurately but also automatically or effortlessly.

The theory of automaticity (LaBerge & Samuels, 1974) begins by noting that all readers have a limited amount of attention, or cognitive resources. Readers must utilize and apply those resources to the two major tasks involved in reading: word recognition and comprehension. The cognitive resources applied to word recognition are not available to be used for comprehension. If readers have to use most of their cognitive resources for word recognition, they have little available for comprehension and, as a result, their comprehension may suffer.

Given the problem of limited attention available to any reader and the dual reading tasks of word recognition and comprehension, one way to maximize the availability of attention for comprehension is to make word recognition processing an automatic as well as accurate process. Automaticity refers to the ability to do a task with minimal effort or with minimal need for attention. When the need for attention in word recognition is minimized, readers are able to employ a maximum amount of attention to the more important task in reading—comprehension. Readers who are automatic in their word recognition usually have reasonably fast, effortless, and confident oral reading. (Although we cannot observe readers' word recognition during silent reading, it is reasonable to expect that the same automatic word recognition process operates during silent reading as well.) Readers who have not achieved automaticity in their reading are usually marked by excessively slow and laborious reading, often stopping at challenging words as the readers attempt to "sound them out." (Again, although we describe a manifestation of lack of automaticity in oral reading, we can expect that the same process occurs during silent reading.) One other characteristic is also apparent in automatic and less-than-automatic reading. Readers who are automatic in word recognition tend to better comprehend what they read compared with readers who have not achieved full automaticity in their reading. Automatic readers are able to devote more of their cognitive resources to making meaning than readers who are less automatic.

To help students achieve automaticity in word recognition, they must practice reading. In reading, practice means consistent contextual reading. Consider all the things that are automatic processes for humans besides reading—cooking a favorite dish in the kitchen, hitting a golf ball, walking around the block, driving a car. For most people, driving an automobile is now a pretty automatic task that does not require a lot of cognitive energy. Yet, such a task was very effortful when first learning to drive. I (Tim) recall being a 16-year-old and having to devote all my attention to the act of driving, lest I have an accident and possibly hurt someone. I had to turn off the radio and anyone in the car with me had to be absolutely quiet. I couldn't be distracted by anyone talking to me. With some practice, however, I developed my driving skills to a point of automaticity. Now I am able to drive accurately (safely) and automatically and at the same time converse with fellow passengers, listen to the radio, and observe the scenery. In reading, we want readers to be so automatic in recognizing the words in a text that they can apply their attention to that all-important task, reading comprehension.

Lack of automaticity in reading can snowball into many other difficulties. Students who are not fully automatic tend to read at a slower pace than more normally developing readers. Slower reading means less reading per given period of time. So a reader who reads at 45 words per minute while more normally developing readers in the class read at 135 words per minute will require 3 additional hours to read the same amount as the more normally developing student can read in 1 hour. Because this reading process is arduous for these slower readers, they may begin to refrain from reading. Then, as these students read less, their automaticity will continue to weaken, their comprehension will suffer, their content knowledge will lag, and their confidence as readers and learners will diminish. Meanwhile, quite the opposite will happen for the more automatic readers. Stanovich (1986) has termed this phenomenon the *Matthew Effect* from the biblical reference from the gospel of Matthew that the rich will get richer while the poor will get poorer. Automaticity is a key to preventing the negative consequences of the Matthew Effect in reading.

In addition to word recognition, teachers also must consider prosody, or expression, in fluency. A fluent reader (or speaker) is not just someone who reads the words in the text accurately and quickly, but also someone who uses his or her voice to aid comprehension and satisfaction for the listener. For example, fluent readers can determine when they should alter cadence, speed, or pauses in their oral reading. Fluent readers also raise and lower their voices appropriately, phrase the text into syntactically appropriate units, and know when to pause for effect, to help establish meaning for themselves and their audience. Consider the following sentence and how a simple emphasis on a different word can alter the meaning:

Maria asked me if she could borrow my new basketball for an hour.

This is a simple declarative sentence that describes an act by Maria. What happens to the implied meaning when a different word is emphasized?

- *Maria* asked me if she could borrow my new basketball for an hour.

   Implied meaning: Maria, and not Jennifer, asked to use my basketball.

- Maria *asked* me if she could borrow my new basketball for an hour.

   Implied meaning: Maria didn't just take my basketball; she requested it.

- Maria asked me if she could borrow my *new* basketball for an hour.

   Implied meaning: I have several basketballs and Maria borrowed the new one.

- Maria asked me if she could borrow my new basketball *for an hour*.

   Implied meaning: Maria would return the basketball in exactly 60 minutes, not 2 hours.

When the reader emphasizes a different word or phrase in the above or other reading selections, it creates an inference—meaning that is not explicitly stated. Prosody, the interpretation of meaning by the reader, allows the reader to comprehend a text at a deeper level that goes beyond what is explicitly stated in the text itself.

Prosody, or expression, also aids the reader in parsing or segmenting the text into meaningful units or phrases. Prosodic cues in oral reading can help readers identify phrase boundaries, which are not always marked by written punctuation (Schreiber, 1980, 1987, 1991; Schreiber & Read, 1980). Prosody enables the reader to infer syntactic information that is not explicitly stated or marked in the actual text.

Though it may be obvious to most readers that prosody is related to oral reading, some of you may be wondering what prosody has to do with silent reading. Prosody can help readers interpret texts both silently and orally. Most proficient adult readers we have surveyed admit that they often hear themselves when they read silently. That internal voice may not be evident to others, but the reader will hear him-/herself as he or she reads. More important, several large-scale studies, ranging from elementary through secondary students, have demonstrated the connection between oral reading prosody and silent reading comprehension (Daane, Campbell, Grigg, Goodman, & Oranje, 2005; Paige, Rasinski, Magpuri-Lavell, 2012; Pinnell et al., 1995; Rasinski, Riki, & Johnston, 2009). In these studies, students were asked to read a grade-appropriate passage orally in their normal manner. The readings were recorded and independent raters were asked to judge the prosodic quality of the reading. The same students were also administered a silent reading comprehension test—passages read silently followed by questions that measured the degree of understanding of the passage. At every grade level, those students whose oral reading prosody was judged to be the highest also had, on average, the highest silent reading comprehension scores. With every drop in oral reading prosody came a corresponding drop in silent reading comprehension. Moreover, at every grade level tested in these studies, a significant number of students exhibited the lowest levels of prosody.

If oral reading prosody is not something that is emphasized in our reading classrooms, we should not be surprised if many of our students struggle with prosodic reading even into the secondary grades. We mentioned earlier that word recognition automaticity is developed through plenty of practice in reading—wide reading and repeated or deep reading. Interestingly, prosody in reading is developed in much the same way—wide reading and especially repeated reading. As students read widely, they encounter different genres and different texts within a given genre that require different elements of prosody and different levels and types of prosody in order to make meaning and read with appropriate expression. As readers read deeply (one text read several times until it can be read well), they come to recognize and embed in their reading features of prosodic reading that allow for and enhance a meaningful and expressive rendering of the text.

We often use the work of performing actors to illustrate how prosody works and, indeed, how it might be taught in schools. Actors constantly engage in repeated reading or rehearsing of a script in order to make a meaningful and satisfying performance for an audience. Through repeated encounters with a text, often under the direction of a stage or film director or coach, actors experiment with various ways of interpreting their texts orally. The actors read through their scripts to develop prosodic readings of new passages not previously seen or read. As they complete multiple readings, they become more adept and proficient in employing prosodic features in their readings.

Although prosody and automaticity are two separate and distinct parts of fluency, they both are developed through the same process—practice. The challenge for teachers is to make wide and deep reading an authentic process where students read a certain number of pages for a real purpose. Asking the students to read to achieve a certain reading speed or to obtain a prize does not seem to be the type of activity one would find outside the classroom. If the purpose of reading fluency instruction is to cover a requisite number of pages or to achieve a certain reading speed, then the teacher and reader are sacrificing the prosody, expression, and perhaps even the meaning and/or comprehension of the reading passages.

FLUENCY MATTERS, OR DOES IT?

You would think with the research connection between both elements of reading fluency and comprehension that fluency should be considered an important and essential element in reading instruction. The sad fact, however, is that many literacy educators have come to dismiss reading fluency as something unimportant and unnecessary for success in reading. Every year, for example, the International Literacy Association sponsors a "What's Hot'" survey of literacy scholars around the world. Various features of reading instruction are presented to the scholars, who are then asked to determine if the feature should be considered a hot topic or not in reading. For the past several years, the scholars have identified reading fluency as one of the few topics in reading that is "not hot." Moreover, these scholars also generally agreed that reading fluency "should not be hot."

How can it be that fluency and fluency instruction can be theoretically and empirically linked to proficient reading and yet be dismissed by literacy scholars? We think the "not hot" label given to fluency can be explained in the way fluency is addressed and interpreted instructionally by many instructional programs in many classrooms around the country. As mentioned earlier, the word recognition automaticity component of fluency is measured in terms of speed of reading. Robust correlations have been found between reading speed and reading comprehension. Readers who read fast tend to be better comprehenders. This finding, however, has come to be interpreted to mean students should be taught to read fast. In many schools across the country, reading speed goals have been set for every elementary grade level. Of course, many well-meaning and dedicated teachers who know that their jobs may depend on having students achieve the preset goals will create or use instruction that is specifically aimed at having students read faster each day. Students chart and graph their reading speed scores and feel a great deal of satisfaction when they see their reading rates improve. The result of such an emphasis, however, is an increase in speed but a decrease in comprehension. If and when teachers make speed the focal point of reading instruction and practices, the students' comprehension will inevitably suffer.

And yet, despite this understanding, speed continues to dominate fluency and overall reading instruction. My colleague and I (Tim) have documented how in many fluency programs the goal for reading speed continues to increase (Rasinski & Hamman, 2010). Some teachers continue to make the hasty leap that if some speed is good, then a higher reading speed is even better. The push for speed has grown so much/exponentially that the normal reading rate 10 or so years ago is now considered below average; those students who read at that rate are considered at risk for failure. Although reading rates have indeed increased over the past decade, overall reading achievement and comprehension levels have remained stagnant.

What teachers, administrators, and students must realize is that although reading speed is a measure of word recognition automaticity, it is not the same as word recognition automaticity. Speed is an outcome of automaticity, not a cause. As readers become more automatic in their word recognition, they become faster in their reading.

Then, as automaticity improves, readers have more of their cognitive resources available for comprehension, so comprehension and speed improve with greater automaticity. Comprehension and speed are both consequences of automaticity.

We surely want our students to improve their reading speeds. But we want them to improve their reading rate the way nearly everyone reading this book became a relatively fast reader—through practice with authentic and engaging reading. The vast majority of us are reasonably fast readers, yet most of us cannot recall any of our teachers ever asking us to read faster than we did the day before. For the vast majority of us, our speed naturally increased as we read more and improved our word recognition automaticity.

The diminishment of fluency has also come from its emphasis on oral reading. Automatic and prosodic fluency can most easily be observed when readers read orally. And so, fluency has come to be associated primarily with oral reading. Indeed, in its review of effective reading practices, the National Reading Panel (2000) specifically identified oral reading as the best approach for teaching fluency. Yet, after the primary grades, we recognize that oral reading takes on a secondary role in the reading curriculum. If oral reading is not the primary goal of reading instruction and fluency is associated with oral reading, then fluency instruction itself cannot and should not be a primary goal of reading instruction.

Although fluency is best observed during oral reading, it must be accepted that what happens in oral reading is a pretty good reflection of what happens during silent reading. As mentioned earlier in this chapter, most proficient readers *do* hear themselves as they silently read. Research has demonstrated that measures of oral reading fluency (both automaticity and prosody) are associated with proficiency in silent reading comprehension. So, by working on oral reading fluency, teachers have a chance to improve their students' silent reading comprehension.

A third reason for fluency's lack of heat is its characterization as a primary-grade competency. Chall's (1996) model of reading development locates fluency as a Stage II competency: one that is developed and mastered in the early stages (primary grade levels) of reading. (The assumption then is that fluency instruction is not required beyond Stage II.)

Granted, in an ideal world, teachers, we hope, should develop the foundations of fluency in the primary grades. However, as students move through the grades, the texts they are asked to read become more linguistically challenging. Students start to read and use longer and more sophisticated words and longer and more-complex sentences. And, because teachers may establish a foundation of fluency in the early grades, they must continue to help students grow in fluency in order to meet the challenges of more-difficult texts. If the texts we ask students to read in grades 4 and beyond are at a 3rd-grade level or below, then students' fluency levels need not increase beyond grade 3. The fact is, however, that fluency development must continue; fluency is not an issue solely for the primary grades. Each student, regardless of his or her grade level, needs to continually increase fluency beyond the primary grades, because research has found that a large portion of struggling readers in the intermediate, middle, and secondary grades manifests inadequate fluency in their reading (Paige, Rasinski, & Magpuri-Lavell, 2012).

A fourth reason that fluency has been dismissed is that it is viewed as a separate part of the reading curriculum. There is time for guided reading, when students read authentic material for authentic purposes and engage in authentic discussions and other responses to their reading, and there is a distinct time for fluency reading, when students read and reread short, often contrived texts for the purpose of reading the passage faster than a previous reading of the same text. During fluency instruction there is little emphasis on meaning, just speed.

If fluency instruction is viewed as an instructional time that is distinct from authentic and meaningful reading then, we agree, it should not be hot. But, fluency *should be* hot. If teachers integrate fluency instruction, in its most authentic and engaging form, with the full reading curriculum as well as other areas of the school curriculum, students will engage in reading practices that will promote fluency and increase students' understanding of the texts they read. In the following chapters you will read how this can actually happen.

WHY FLUENCY SHOULD MATTER FOR ALL READERS

Even though fluency may not be viewed by many as hot, teachers should not give up on it. We would hate to see it disappear from the school reading curriculum as it did a hundred years ago. Why should fluency matter?

Research has shown that reading fluency is related to comprehension and overall reading proficiency. Fluency is necessary for comprehension to occur. Without fluency, reading comprehension becomes difficult. This in itself should be a sufficient reason why fluency should matter, why it should be hot.

But there are at least two other reasons why fluency should matter. First, the Common Core State Standards (CCSS) for literacy, the current national guide for literacy instruction in the United States, has identified reading fluency as a "foundational standard." Any structure that is built to last must have a strong foundation. So it is with reading. Schools must work to develop readers who are lifelong and proficient readers. In order to achieve this goal, fluency is an important part of the foundation. Although most of the literacy standards identified in the CCSS deal with various forms of comprehension and close reading, fluency is a competency that underlies all comprehension and close reading. Indeed, the CCSS notes the need for students to successfully negotiate complex texts. Complex texts are challenging texts not only in terms of their content but also in terms of their linguistic features—more-complex sentences, more-challenging vocabulary, and so forth. Fluency clearly plays a role in helping students read and understand the more complex texts that they will encounter in the coming years.

Second, students who perform poorly on the high-stakes reading comprehension tests that have become part and parcel of school curricula throughout the United States exhibit a lack of fluency. In Valencia and Buly's (2004) aptly titled article "Behind Test Scores: What Struggling Readers Really Need," they examined the performance of 5th-grade students who performed below the standard on a state reading examination. They found that well over half of the students manifested difficulties in some aspect of reading fluency. In our own ongoing research of 3rd-grade students who perform below the cut score on a state silent reading proficiency test, we have found more than half of the students exhibit significant difficulties in some aspect of fluency.

CLOSING COMMENTS

If difficulties in reading fluency are associated with poor reading comprehension and poor performance on silent reading comprehension tests, then it would seem reasonable to assume that instruction to improve reading fluency may lead to improved reading comprehension. In essence, such instruction may help students cross that metaphorical bridge from word recognition to reading comprehension. In the coming chapters, we will share with you fluency instructional strategies that lead to improvements in reading fluency, reading comprehension, and overall reading proficiency.

THINK ABOUT IT

Prosody is important. Think about the last time you listened to someone speak in a monotone, word-by-word, robotic style without enthusiasm or confidence. What was your response to having to listen to this person? Our guess is that you, like us, found the listening difficult—not only to pay attention to but also to actually make meaning from the person's speech. Now, think about listening to someone who spoke with expression, phrasing, enthusiasm, and confidence. Was your response different?

WHAT WE THINK

We think the same phenomenon occurs while reading. As we read, if our inner voice processes the text in a slow, halting, and unenthusiastic manner, our comprehension will be hindered. On the other hand, when we read something and we feel that our inner voice is confident and expressive, our understanding of the text tends to improve. Prosody, or expression while reading, is important.

CHAPTER 3

If Fluency Matters, Where Do We Start? Let's Try Assessment

In Chapter 2 we argued that fluency does matter when it comes to learning to read proficiently and is something we need to be concerned about. But how do we know that it matters in your school, in your classroom, and with your students? The only way we can tell if fluency is an issue and if our instruction is leading to improvements in students' reading performance is through measuring or assessing reading fluency. In this chapter, we explore some simple but powerful ways to assess fluency and to diagnose students who may be experiencing difficulty with fluency.

WORD RECOGNITION

Let's return a minute to our 3rd-graders Jason and Hamad and their five classmates who are in the intervention group. While Jason and Hamad are off receiving targeted instruction for decoding and word recognition, what is happening with the other five readers whose river, or flow of reading, is not flowing smoothly? As we recall, Mrs. Radovitch has not observed that these children have any particular problems in ultimately sounding out unfamiliar words. She gives them all a grade-level passage to read in order to further assess their oral reading. As they read the words in the passage, she notes the ease with which they decode the words. Although they struggle with some of the words and have to slow down or stop to sound them out, they tend to be successful in word decoding, so she affirms that word decoding is not the problem. Three of the students read the grade-level passage within the acceptable range (95% of words are read accurately) and two are approaching it. These students have, as they say, "broken the code." Yet their flow or ease of oral reading is fraught with obstacles that impact meaning. For example, when the students read, they ignore ending punctuation and stumble from one sentence to the next. Sometimes, they "robot read," delivering each word individually and devoid of any semblance of expression or confidence. And, sometimes, the students read with inappropriate pacing—they speed up when they know the words and slow down or stop when they don't. Moreover, although these students tend to read the words accurately, their comprehension of the passage, and other grade-level passages, is poor. The reading difficulty these students are having appears to go beyond mere word recognition accuracy; Mrs. Radovitch feels that perhaps one or more aspects of fluency such as poor pacing, laborious word decoding, and lack of expression are contributing to these students' difficulty in reading.

IDENTIFYING THE PROBLEM

In order to unveil what issues are affecting these students' fluency, the teacher must first determine the nature of the difficulty the students are experiencing. Typically, the first indication a teacher in Mrs. Radovitch's situation may get that a student is struggling with fluency is by listening to her students read aloud in regular class settings. Some teachers might start with traditional approaches like round-robin reading. In this method of instructional group reading, students are called upon in a predetermined order to read a specified portion of a text aloud. The other students, who are waiting for their turns, are asked to follow along silently with the reader. The purpose of round-robin is to give all students an opportunity to read and to monitor each student's reading.

Unfortunately, readers who struggle with texts still have difficulty with instructional and assessment approaches like round-robin, because it highlights students' reading deficiencies in front of the whole class. For example, struggling students who are not as fluent as their proficient peers might lose their place because the proficient peers might read too quickly for less proficient readers. Also, and perhaps most disturbing, the less fluent students might be terrified of reading out loud in front of their peers because of public shame. Unfortunately, the practice is still prevalent in many schools.

IF NOT ROUND-ROBIN READING, THEN WHAT?

Another approach to identifying reading difficulties is to examine the tests that are routinely administered to students. You may be familiar with several of the commercial standardized assessments such as the group administered Stanford Diagnostic Reading Test (SDRT) or the individually administered Woodcock Reading Mastery Test (WRMT-III). Both assessments do a good job of pinpointing reading difficulties and leading to instructional interventions. However, they only provide information based on the product of a student's reading, not the actual reading itself.

Nonstandardized reading assessments, such as informal reading inventories (IRIs), running records (Clay, 2000), and miscue analysis (Goodman, Watson, & Burke, 2005) are less formal in nature and are based on the teacher's ability to interpret the reading behaviors they record. Hybrid versions of informal assessments and commercial standardized tests, such as *Developmental Reading Assessment* (Beaver, Carter, Sreenivasan, Leon, & Siburt, 2004) and the *Qualitative Reading Inventory* (Leslie & Caldwell, 2011), also include a strong informal, teacher-interpretation component. Most of these assessments provide teachers with an in-depth view of their students as readers—their level of achievement and, to some extent, their various strengths and areas of concern in reading. We acknowledge and honor the amount of information the above assessments provide.

Now that Mrs. R has identified a potential problem, what does she do? Is there anything she can do to confirm her suspicions without having to give a lengthy test to each student? We think there are indeed strategies Mrs. Radovitch can implement in her classroom that don't involve a great deal of precious instructional time. Read on to see what she found that worked for her.

In an elementary school reading publication, Mrs. Radovitch read about a simple, efficient, and informal method of measuring fluency. The article was backed by research indicating that reading fluency was highly correlated to silent reading comprehension and introduced an innovative method: the 3-Minute Reading Assessment (3MRA). The 3MRA (Rasinski & Padak, 2005a, 2005b) is used primarily as a screening and diagnostic reading assessment. It provides teachers with information on a student's reading ability in the areas of word recognition (decoding), fluency (word recognition automaticity and prosody), and comprehension. One of the most appealing features of the 3MRA is that it can be administered to a student in a matter of minutes.

THINK ABOUT IT

You may be familiar with some or all of these assessments. You may have given them yourself or, in the case of the SDRT and WRMT-III, may simply have had the results given to you to make sense of them as best you could. Take a minute and list any concerns you have about employing these tests classwide for assessing fluency. If you were to pick one concern major with these assessments, what would it be?

WHAT WE THINK

We think if there is one major drawback common to these sorts of assessments, it can be summed up in one word: time. These and many of the other formal and informal reading assessments available to teachers take considerable time to prepare, administer, score, and interpret. For example, the full-scale administration of one of the aforementioned informal reading inventories can take 1 to 2 hours to give to a student and another hour to score and interpret. Although the data collections teachers obtain from such assessments are valid and valuable, the time needed to complete them makes them almost impossible to administer to every student in the classroom. Nevertheless, we are seeing instances in many schools in which teachers are expected to administer an informal reading inventory to every student at least two, if not three, times a year. If each teacher attempted to administer this 1- to 3-hour test to a class with approximately 25 students, it would take him or her at least 25 to 75 hours to complete; that's up to 3 weeks of school. And this would take away instructional time for teaching and reading.

The premise of 3MRA is simple. A student reads a relatively short grade-level or near-grade-level passage, usually between 100 and 200 words for 1 minute, while the teacher follows along with a copy of the text. As the student reads, the teacher listens closely to the reading and marks any uncorrected word recognition errors. The teacher also marks where the student is in the text after 1 minute of reading. At the end of the reading, the text is removed from the student's view and he or she is asked to retell or summarize what he or she just read.

From this data, the teacher is able to obtain information on several reading competencies. First, the teacher can infer the student's word recognition *accuracy* by the percentage of words read correctly in the passage (instructional level is considered 92–98% words read correctly). In addition to accuracy, the teacher can ascertain the student's word recognition *automaticity* by the number of words read correctly in the first minute of reading (WCPM). (The teacher should use each student's WCPM score and then compare it to the student's grade level and time-of-year norms [Figure 3.1].) This should help the teacher determine if the student is on track in this competency.

The WCPM scores presented in Figure 3.1 are roughly reading rates that represent the 50th percentile (or normal) score for readers at various grade levels. Reading rate or speed is a good indicator of word recognition automaticity. Scores significantly below the identified range of rates may indicate that fluency (word recognition automaticity) is a concern for the student.

One of the rather unique features of the 3MRA approach is that it measures prosody, or expressiveness, in oral reading, a component of fluency that is often neglected. In their review of fluency research, Kuhn, Schwanenflugel, Meisinger, Levy, and Rasinski (2010) noted:

> Fluency combines accuracy, automaticity, and oral reading prosody, which, taken together, facilitate the reader's construction of meaning. It is demonstrated during oral reading through ease of word recognition, appropriate pacing, phrasing, and intonation. It is a factor in both oral and silent reading that can limit or support comprehension. (p. 240)

Once the teacher has used Figure 3.1 to determine word recognition automaticity on the 3MRA, he or she can then refer to a five-factor rubric to help determine prosody and overall expressiveness.

Figure 3.1. Oral Reading Fluency (Automaticity) Target-Rate Norms by Grade

Grade	Fall (WCPM)	Winter (WCPM)	Spring (WCPM)
1	5–10	10–50	30–90
2	30–80	50–100	70–130
3	50–110	70–120	80–140
4	70–120	80–130	90–140
5	80–130	90–140	100–150
6	90–140	100–150	110–160
7	100–150	110–160	120–170
8	110–160	120–180	130–180

Sources: Rasinski, T., & Padak, N. (2005a, 2005b). Used with permission from Scholastic.

In a five-factor rubric (Figure 3.2), total scores at or above 12 indicate that the student is reading with appropriate prosody, while scores below 12 may indicate that prosody may be a concern that requires some additional instruction and guidance.

Finally, comprehension can be assessed by rating each student's oral retelling of the passage against a six-point rubric (Figure 3.3).

Figure 3.2. Multidimensional Fluency Rubric

Use the following scales to rate reader fluency on the dimensions of expression and volume, phrasing, smoothness, and pace.

A. Expression

1. Reads with little or no expression or enthusiasm in voice. Reads words as if simply to get them out. Little sense of trying to make text sound like natural language. Tends to read in a quiet voice.
2. Some expression. Begins to use voice to make text sound like natural language in some areas of the text, but not others. Focus remains largely on saying the words. Still reads in a voice that is quiet.
3. Sounds like natural language throughout the better part of the passage. Occasionally slips into expressionless reading. Voice volume is generally appropriate throughout the text.
4. Reads with good expression and enthusiasm throughout the text. Sounds like natural language. Reader is able to vary expression and volume to match his or her interpretation of the passage.

B. Volume & Confidence

1. Reads in a very quiet voice (as if not wanting to read). May have to be prompted to read a bit louder. Appears to have no confidence in him-/herself as a reader.
2. Volume is slightly louder, though not at a level considered appropriate. Oral reading continues to demonstrate a lack of confidence in him-/herself as a reader.
3. Voice volume is generally appropriate throughout the text. Appears to have some degree of confidence in him-/herself.
4. Reads with a strong volume that reflects a high degree of confidence in him-/herself as a reader.

C. Phrasing & Intonation

1. Monotonic with little sense of phrase boundaries; frequent word-by-word reading.
2. Frequent short phrases giving the impression of choppy reading; improper stress and intonation that fail to mark ends of sentences and clauses.
3. Mixture of run-ons, mid-sentence pauses for breath, and possibly some choppiness; reasonable stress/intonation.

Figure continues on next page

Figure 3.2. Multidimensional Fluency Rubric *(continued)*

4. Generally well phrased; reads mostly in clause and sentence units with adequate attention to expression.

D. Smoothness

1. Frequent extended pauses, hesitations, false starts, sound-outs, repetitions, and/or multiple attempts.
2. Several "rough spots" in text where extended pauses, hesitations, and so on are more frequent and disruptive.
3. Occasional breaks in smoothness caused by difficulties with specific words and/or structures.
4. Generally smooth reading with some breaks, but word and structure difficulties are resolved quickly, usually through self-correction.

E. Pace (during sections of minimal disruption)

1. Slow and laborious.
2. Moderately slow.
3. Uneven mixture of fast and slow reading.
4. Consistently conversational.

Scores range from 5 to 20. Total scores below 12 may indicate that fluency may be a concern. Scores of 12 or above indicate that the student is at or above a minimal grade level of fluency for the passage read.

Note. Adapted from T. V. Rasinski, 2010, *The Fluent Reader* (2nd ed.), New York, NY: Scholastic. Used with permission.

Figure 3.3. Comprehension Rubric

1. No recall or minimal recall of only a fact of two from the passage.
2. Recall of a number of unrelated facts of varied importance.
3. Recall of the main idea of the passage with a few supporting details.
4. Recall of the main idea along with a fairly robust set of supporting details, although his or her information is not necessarily organized logically or sequentially as presented in the passage.
5. Recall is a comprehensive summary of the passage, presented in a logical order and/or with a robust set of details and that includes a statement of the main idea.
6. Recall is a comprehensive summary of the passage, presented in a logical order and/or with a robust or full set of details and that includes a statement of the main idea. Student makes reasonable connections beyond the text to his or her own personal life and beyond.

Scores of 3 or above indicate adequate comprehension or higher. Scores of 1 or 2 indicate that the student did not have adequate comprehension of the passage.

Ms. Radovitch has previously discerned that word decoding is not the major roadblock for her struggling readers. The problem seems to be when the students read connected text. Students' oral reading of grade-level texts is marked by slow, laborious, and inexpressive reading. Poor comprehension is also noted. If fluent reading is being able to read connected text accurately, but also at a good pace with appropriate expression and adequate comprehension, these students do not appear to be fluent readers.

WORD RECOGNITION AUTOMATICITY
AND THE QUESTION OF SPEED

Ms. Radovitch administers the 3MRA to her other five students. As Ms. Radovitch administers the test, she is aware that some of her pupils have already been conditioned to believe that oral reading means fast reading. So, when she asks them to read for the 3MRA, she reminds them not to hurry; she wants their best oral reading, not their fastest. To help ensure that her students process the information/take their time, she asks students to read as if they were telling the story to someone. At no time during the test does she discuss reading rate with them. Instead of focusing on their scores, she compliments them for reading the passage well.

Though we agree that reading speed is an important measure of oral reading fluency (word recognition automaticity), it is a by-product of fluent reading. Through plenty of reading practice students become automatic in their word recognition. Automaticity leads to two outcomes—readers now have additional cognitive capacity to make meaning and readers are able to read the words in a passage more quickly.

Past research that correlated oral reading rate with silent comprehension (Fuchs, Fuchs, Hosp, & Jenkins, 2001; Jenkins, Fuchs, van den Broek, Espin, & Deno, 2003) was unfortunately interpreted to infer that comprehension and word recognition automaticity could be increased by getting struggling readers to simply try to read faster and rewarding them accordingly. Although the correlation between oral reading rate and silent reading comprehension is quite strong, we know of no compelling research that indicates a causal relationship between the two. In other words, you don't make struggling readers comprehend better by encouraging them to read as fast as they can. What does seem to be effective for increasing silent reading comprehension among disfluent readers is instruction that encourages them to read at a natural pace with the kind of inflection we use in everyday speech and that reflects meaning (Miller & Schwanenflugel, 2008).

When good readers read naturally, they are mindful of the punctuation cues and implicit phrasing that bring meaning to a text. We understand, of course, that we all read faster when we read silently, but it doesn't mean we are oblivious to those same cues. In fact, recent research suggests just the opposite. Measuring brain activity and eye movements of subjects when reading aloud, Steinhauer (2003) found that good readers exhibit a distinct inner voice while reading—one that is processing the expressive boundaries in natural speech and dividing the text into meaningful phrases beyond the written punctuation. The importance of this finding cannot be overstated. Essentially, this means that proficient readers comprehend well when they read because they read with expression, whether they are reading orally for someone else or silently by themselves.

There is little reason to believe that readers who read like robots (word-for-word) or like NASCAR racers (quickly, at breakneck speeds) when reading orally are reading with good internal expression and comprehension when they read silently. However, fluent readers,

THINK ABOUT IT

What do you do when you are reading a more complex text silently and come across sentences that are 40 or 50 words long with minimal punctuation? If you don't remember, try this one: "This logical formulation is coterminous with political demonstration, overcoming the temporal lag time that separates the syllogism from action" (Lewis, 2012, p. 122).

WHAT WE THINK

We think that after the first time through, you probably went back and read the complex text again, this time trying to figure out where commas or pauses would help. If you are like me (Jim), you also might have whispered quietly while reading to see if hearing the sentence would help you make sense of it. The point is, we clarify text by hearing it in our heads and listening to the voices embedded in the text. Students who struggle with reading comprehension often have difficulty in reading with an expression that reflects and enhances the meaning of the passage.

being freed from having to laboriously form sounds and words during oral and silent reading, can shift into overdrive, grouping words into meaningful phrases with appropriate expression, at higher rates of speed and with enhanced comprehension.

Not surprisingly, Mrs. Radovitch finds her five students reading well below the grade-level norms for word recognition automaticity as measured by reading rate (Figure 3.1). Word recognition automaticity is obviously an issue that is inhibiting fluency and comprehension. She also realizes some key issues about her students' expressiveness from the Multidimensional Fluency Rubric. Previously, she speculated that these students might have difficulties with the expressive oral reading component of fluency; now, however, after the administering, scoring, and interpreting of the 3MRA, she had specific data about their expression, volume, phrasing, smoothness, and pacing during oral readings. All of her five students exhibited difficulty in one or more areas of expression.

Now that she knew her students' strengths and weaknesses, she could modify and target her lessons to help her students improve in fluency and their overall reading ability. For example, each student demonstrated weakness in one or more of the competencies covered in the Multidimensional Fluency Rubric. So, Mrs. R decided to tailor her instruction to meet the specific needs of each student. Over the next few months, she continued to modify her lessons and gave her students the 3MRAs to monitor their growth in various aspects of reading (comprehension, fluency, and so on).

For example, Jamar scored low in dimensions of Volume & Confidence and Pace. His oral reading was slow and laborious, barely audible, and he was extremely shy about reading aloud even in the absence of peers. Mrs. Radovitch decided that to increase his confidence, she would echo read with him. Echo reading is where a proficient reader—in this case, Mrs. Radovitch—takes text at the student's independent level and scaffolds the student to independent prosodic reading.

Mrs. R chose a high-interest story with dialogue and told Jamar that they were going to read part of a story together. She explained that she would start reading and after every sentence it would be his job to read the same sentence the same way she did, echoing her. After a few sentences, she said, "You've been reading these sentences really well. Read the next sentence to yourself. Can you hear in your head how I would say it? Go ahead now and read it out loud the way you think I would read it." After he read, she complimented him on his expression and said they were going to do a few more.

As Jamar's confidence began to increase, Mrs. Radovitch announced that they were going to make it more interesting by playing a game called the Controlled Shouting Match. The routine was the same as echo reading but she informed him that now they were going to stand up and face each other while reading. Jamar was instructed to listen carefully to how loud Mrs. R read. If she read even a little louder, he was to take a step back and read the line she just read, with the same volume. Mrs. R increased her volume significantly about every other line. And of course, every few lines she stopped and allowed him to read the next sentence to himself and then the way he thought she would read it, now with the appropriate volume as well. As fun as the game was, Mrs. Radovitch knew better than to wear it out and limited the echo reading to about 10 minutes. The next day, to warm up, she began by asking Jamar to pick up where they had left off, repeating the echo reading of the previous day. But then, after complimenting him on how well he was doing, she told him they were ready to switch roles. She would echo him, reading exactly the way he did. Almost immediately they began to play the Controlled Shouting Match, this time with him leading. As Jamar's confidence improved and his volume increased, she integrated him into a short Readers Theatre script with some of his peers. When she introduced the script, she had the whole small cast echo read with her the first time through, something Jamar was familiar with. She found that within a week there was noticeable improvement in both his confidence and volume.

In her subsequent echo reading sessions with him, she reminded him that when good readers read to themselves they read faster than when they read out loud even as they hear the voice in their head. And when they read aloud they are always "thinking ahead to get the sound right, so that eventually they don't even have to slow down to do it."

Brandon had a different challenge. Though his volume and confidence were good, he had low scores in the Pace, Phasing, & Intonation and Smoothness dimensions. His problem was that he slowed to a crawl during some sections and raced through any parts he could at breakneck speed, as if to make up for lost time. His reading was mostly devoid of expression. The result was a mixture of fast and slow reading, similar to the driving of an aggressive driver in moderately heavy traffic.

Mrs. R discerned that previous instruction had led Brandon to be-lieve that his job while reading aloud was to read as fast as he possibly could, so every time he slowed down, it was necessary to hurry up to get back into the race. Not surprisingly, Brandon's comprehension scores were correspondingly low.

Working with Brandon, Mrs. R modeled three short read-alouds. Asking him to listen for the difference in the way she read, her first rendition was slow and monotonic with frequent word-by-word read-ing. Her second rendition was equally without expression but very fast and choppy, slowing down and speeding up at inappropriate places. The third rendition she read with slightly exaggerated expression. Asking him to compare the renditions, they came up with the name of "The Robot" for the first, monotonic, word-by-word reading. For the second time she read, where her pace was inconsistent and phrasing illogical, they chose to call it "The Race Car in Traffic." Finally, for the last, slightly exaggerated version, they agreed upon "The Actor."

She asked Brandon how he thought "Actors" knew how to read the way they did and he was surprised to learn that they read the way they did because they knew what the sentence meant and repeated the voice they heard in their head. With this in mind, she worked with Brandon to help him monitor his oral reading to strive at sounding like "The Actor." She emphasized that there was no need to rush and eliminated obvious timings from his reading instruction. For Brandon, she found some short, humorous poems written especially with boys in mind and transitioned him to short, age-appropriate monologues.

As with Jamar, Mrs. R reminded Brandon that good readers hear their voice even when they are reading silently. Not surprisingly, as Brandon's oral reading became more "Actor-like," his comprehension scores began to increase. Casting both boys in a Readers Theatre pro-duction a few weeks later, Mrs. Radovitch provided the opportunity for Jamar and Brandon to combine their new talents in a form that reinforced the improvements both had made independently.

CAVEATS AND CHALLENGES IN ASSESSING FLUENCY

Although, in the past, teachers have given students their assessment scores, doing so might give students the wrong focus. If children par-ticipate in charting their word recognition automaticity progress, they might get the impression that speed is the goal. Instead, teachers should monitor students' progress, but refrain from allowing students to focus on reading rate. When teachers give students kudos for increases on reading rate alone, students are likely to come to the conclusion that they should read as fast as they can. These students are inevitably products of the misunderstanding that speed of oral reading produces fluency. Though appropriate pacing (speed) is a measure of one component of reading fluency—word recognition automaticity—it is not a measure of prosody, or expressiveness, while reading. Thus, we suggest that teachers limit sharing with students their reading rate data. It may be encouraging for students to see their rate grow, but it can also give them the wrong impression of what speed reflects and lead students to ignore expression in reading.

Reading with expression enhances higher-level thinking skills that require the student to put words into meaningful phrases in order to make sense of the text. Students who read with good expression have been shown to score better on measures of silent reading comprehension (Paige, Rasinski, & Magpuri-Lavell, 2012; Rasinski et al., 2005; Rasinski, Riki, & Johnston, 2009). Thus, understanding and monitoring prosody, or expression, is essential. Often seen as merely an assessment add-on to a students' oral reading rate, expression, or prosody, is actually as good, if not a better, indicator of silent reading comprehension. Recent research indicates *how* the student is reading aloud is importantly linked to how well he or she comprehends when reading silently (Miller & Schwanenflugel, 2008).

Punctuation, with the exception of the question mark and exclamation point, are very basic speed indicators. A period is understood as a longer pause and a comma, as a shorter pause. Generally speaking, there is no punctuation to signal a gradual stop, a change in pitch or intonation, or a final phrase rising, falling, or lengthening. But good oral readers do this. Ask actors how they know how to read a line and you'll hear things like, "I read through [the script] once to get a lay of the land and ask myself, 'What is going on here? What is being conveyed?' Then I hear an inner voice and start to vocalize it."

If teachers want to give their students an impression of what's important in oral reading, they should emphasize comprehension and meaningful expression. Frequent modeling and explicit instruction in how good oral readers do what they do will transfer to the inner prosody that Steinhauer (2003) found exists in skilled readers. Thus, when teachers approach assessment of fluency, they should make expression, or prosody, an equal partner with word recognition automaticity (reading rate) in order to gain a full measure of fluency and gain better insight into what may be causing students difficulty in their reading.

In order to assess to establish a fluency benchmark, we suggest using the 16-point Multidimensional Fluency Rubric (Figure 3.2) to easily and quickly assess where a student falls on the fluency spectrum. The use of the rubric gives the teacher the ability to monitor progress in fluency. Moreover, unlike reading rate data, sharing data on students' growth in the elements of prosody with students themselves is quite appropriate. Students' attention and focus need to be placed on factors that enhance fluency and comprehension.

Clearly, it is important for students to have a good understanding of the nature of fluency itself. Some teachers take a version of the Multidimensional Fluency Rubric and make it "kid-friendly"—enlarge it and post it in the room—to help students make connections to it. By making it easily viewable, teachers can refer to the chart when they discuss fluency. Then, the students also can judge the quality of their own oral and silent reading skills along the dimension of the posted rubric. Through such regular self-assessment, students will develop a better metacognitive awareness of the importance of fluency and the factors that lead to improved fluency and comprehension.

CLOSING COMMENTS

If fluency is indeed important, then teachers need to have ways to measure it that do not take an excessive amount of time or energy. We feel that the best and most empowering approach to fluency assessment is for teachers to listen to students read and then, using their own skill as an assessor, rate their reading along various dimensions deemed important for fluency. When teachers have a better understanding of the nature of fluency and how it is measured, they will be more able to direct their energy and efforts toward improving fluency in their students and themselves.

CHAPTER 4

Teaching Fluency: Back to the Future

If you are old enough, you may remember time spent in elementary school engaging in oral recitation. Perhaps it was a famous speech from American history (e.g., Lincoln's Gettysburg Address or excerpts from Patrick Henry's "Give Me Liberty or Give Me Death" speech) or an important cultural poem (e.g., "Oh Captain! My Captain!" by Walt Whitman), or perhaps even a significant section from a story during class. In all of these cases, you were expected to read your assigned piece with appropriate expression and volume. The purpose of doing oral recitation was to help students develop their confidence and expression when they read orally.

In this chapter, we identify key instructional strategies for improving both components of reading fluency—automatic word recognition and prosody. Until the National Reading Panel (2000) identified fluency as a critical reading competency, few instructional reading programs included fluency as a major learning objective. In reality, though, reading fluency has been an integral part of formal reading instruction in America since colonial times.

In colonial days, the number of readers and the amount of reading material available in any household was limited. For most families, reading often occurred when one family member read orally to the rest of the family. Fluent oral reading was considered a goal for classroom instruction because of its prominence in people's daily lives for entertainment and sharing information. If others were to enjoy a book, newspaper, or other text, someone had to read aloud fluently.

Later, as reading (comprehension) became more commonplace, the role of reading fluency diminished. Most assumed that teaching oral reading fluency was not necessary because the goal of reading instruction was primarily (silent) reading comprehension. These two reading goals of reading comprehension and fluent oral reading seemed diametrically opposed. As fluency was diminished in importance, instruction in fluency also diminished; students don't learn unless we teach them.

Thankfully, however, teachers and scholars discovered that (oral) reading fluency was a necessary (but not sufficient) condition for proficient (silent) reading comprehension. Fluency is important for comprehension. Even the Common Core State Standards identify fluency as foundational for reading success. Moreover, we have found that difficulties in fluency plague many students and appear to be a major source of difficulty in reading comprehension. Fluency needs to be taught, and we can look to past practices to find how it can be taught.

READ ALOUD

Today, for many students, reading fluency is nothing more than trying to read as fast as they can. Last year, we interviewed some 1st-graders toward the end of the school year in one of our local schools. We asked individual students, "Who is the best reader in your class?" Once they named that student, we then asked them, "What makes that student such a good reader?" The students explained that the classmate they chose as the best reader was so good because he or she read fast.

A few months ago, in our reading clinic, we had a 2nd-grader who was asked to read a passage from an informal reading inventory. Before beginning to read, the student looked up at the clinician and asked in a very sincere voice, "Should I read this as fast as I can?" Stunned at students' focus on speed, we began to wonder from where these questions came. We assume that these student observations might be the result of fluency instruction, which focuses on students reading timed passages as quickly as they can, and weekly fluency assessments, which involve determining the number of words in a passage students can read correctly in a minute. With the focus on these types of assessments, it is not difficult to see how young students can translate these experiences into an internal definition of proficient reading.

Yet, although maintaining appropriate rate while reading is a part of fluency, it is not the most important part. Instead of focusing on fluency through speed, we encourage teachers to focus on fluency through meaningful and appropriate expression, volume, and rate that reflects and adds to the meaning of the passage

MODELING FLUENT READING

What better way for students to develop a mental model of fluency than through that age-old activity called teacher read-aloud? During those precious 10–15 minutes right before or after lunch (or some other special time during the day) when the teacher reads a storybook to the class, he or she is providing a model of what fluent reading is like. The teacher is employing those prosodic elements just mentioned to capture students' interest and add to the meaning of the story. Never once in this method is the focus speed; thus, students can see and hear the importance of alternate strategies, rather than just speed.

We know that read-aloud of any sort is valuable. Research indicates that reading to children regularly improves reading comprehension and increases students' vocabulary (Rasinski, 2010). Read-aloud also improves students' attitude toward books and reading and provides teachers with an ideal time to model authentic fluent reading for students.

We read aloud often to students (our college students as well as elementary students, when we are in the schools). First of all, read-aloud is a great way to begin or end an instructional session. After read-alouds, we can open doors for further discussion about the text. For example, when we are done reading, we can talk for a few minutes about the text we just read and ask students to make inferences or predictions about characters and future events in the story. However, we also sometimes chat with our students about the way we read or performed the story itself. We might ask questions like these:

- Did you notice how I changed my voice when I read the part of a different character? Did that help you understand the story a little better?
- What were you thinking when I sped up my reading at this section? (The teacher might model rereading the section again to ensure clarity.)
- What did you like about my voice as I read to you? What didn't you like?
- What do you think I had to do in order to be able to read the story in a voice that you enjoyed?

Questions like these help focus students' attention on a part of the read-aloud that often goes unnoticed. Even as adults, we are often so invested in the plot of the story that we may not notice how the reader is using his or her voice to enhance the listening experience.

Occasionally when we read to students, we will purposely embed in our voices elements that detract from fluency—we may read without or with minimal expression; or read in a slow, word-by-word manner; or read at an excessively fast pace, ignoring most punctuation; or read in a very soft, almost inaudible voice; or hesitate on some words; or even mispronounce some words. Whether it is conscious or subconscious, readers engage in these techniques to ensure that they maintain their audience's attention.

To help students understand the importance of these elements in fluency, we try to model some sentences that are read "poorly." To start, we typically begin by reading one to two sentence(s) for the students and then stop. Then, we ask students to comment on our reading. They usually say it wasn't very good. We ask next what made it not very good, and of course, the students quickly pinpoint the errors in our oral reading. Once they determine the word recognition errors, we ask them what our not-so-good reading did for them. (This is when the "aha" moment comes.) The students will note that our marginal reading detracted from their understanding and satisfaction with the story. We use the students' feedback as a bridge to explain why expression is so vital to their reading. Our next point to students is this: If we read in a manner that lacks fluency in some way and you don't enjoy or understand the passage as well as if it were read in a more fluent and expressive voice, then you need to try to make your own independent reading as fluent and expressive as possible. That way, you won't have difficulty understanding the text and/or you won't find the text uninteresting.

Reading aloud to students is not the same as the students reading on their own. However, read-aloud is important because it provides students with a model of how they themselves should read. (Of course, we are assuming that when all teachers read to their students they are able to read with good fluency.)

ASSISTED READING

Most learning experiences are aided when the learner is provided with a model of what it is that he or she is supposed to learn or do. Similarly, learning is also facilitated when students are offered assistance by their teachers, who model reading fluency for them and also read with students. Recall how after watching your parents drive your family car for years, you were finally given your learner's permit. However, before you could go solo, you had to drive for several weeks or months with a more experienced driver sitting next to you in the front seat, providing guidance and assistance as needed. This principle of learning applies to reading fluency as well.

After hearing fluent readers read, students need opportunities to read while at the same time being guided or provided assistance while reading. This takes the form of novice reader reading a text while simultaneously hearing the same text read fluently by a more advanced reader or readers. By hearing the fluent rendering of a text while simultaneously doing his or her best to read, the novice reader will begin to approximate the more fluent reading.

Choral Reading

Probably the most common form of assisted reading is choral reading, where a group of readers read one text aloud together. Assuming that at least some of the readers in the choral reading group are more fluent than others (more often than not, the teacher will include him- or herself in the choral reading group), the less fluent readers will benefit from hearing the fluent reading of the same text. We see choral reading done often in the primary grades. It is a wonderful opportunity to bring a group together to work as a team or to share a custom (e.g., the Pledge of Allegiance). Moreover, it is a chance to improve students' reading fluency. Recent research by David Paige (2011, in press) suggests that choral reading can even facilitate the reading fluency development of upper elementary and middle school students.

Think of the wonderful texts that can easily be read (or sung) chorally. These include poems, song lyrics, segments of famous speeches, and pledges. In addition to language arts classes, Paige suggests that students can also read segments of texts that are used for instruction in social studies or science classes. Whether the students are in math or science, elementary or high school, the critical key for choral reading is that the written text be made available for students and that they be prompted to track the text visually as they read. Texts such as the Pledge of Allegiance are not as effective because they are performed daily to the point at which students have the text memorized and do not have to actually read the text. Although this may be a choral performance, it is not choral reading. Students should not be as familiar with the text, so their eyes stay on the print being performed; this way, the teacher may assume that reading will occur.

Partner Choral Reading

When two readers read a text together and one reader is more fluent than the other, partner choral reading is taking place. Various forms of partner choral reading go by the names Neurological Impress Reading; paired reading; and dyad, or buddy, reading. In each case, a less fluent reader sits side by side with a more fluent reader. The more fluent reader can be a teacher, an adult aide, or a volunteer in the classroom; a parent or other adult at home; or even a fellow student. Once the reading pair is established, both readers read the same text orally, with one of the readers physically pointing to the text as it is read. The text can be of any type and any level of difficulty. As the two individuals read together, however, it appears that the less fluent reader is able to make maximum gains in fluency and comprehension when the text is a bit challenging, a text that the less fluent reader would have difficulty reading on his or her own. A number of studies have demonstrated partner choral reading to have great potential for improving the reading performance, including comprehension, of the less fluent reader (e.g., Eldredge & Butterfield, 1986; Eldredge & Quinn, 1988; Heckelman, 1969). In one case, slightly over 7 hours of partner choral reading, done in 15-minute increments over 6 weeks, resulted in one student improving his reading performance by nearly six grade levels! When the two individuals read the passage together, the reading session should last approximately 10–15 minutes. When the two partners read in this way, it can be a fairly intensive activity for both readers, so the teacher will want to keep each partner reading session reasonably short in length.

Technology and Assisted Reading

Of course, you don't have to have a live person sitting next to you for assisted reading to occur. Have you ever read a book or other text while simultaneously listening to a recorded oral version of the same text? If so, you did a form of assisted reading. Technology offers some ways to expand how assisted reading can take place.

One of the very first studies of reading fluency used a form of technology-assisted reading. In her seminal article entitled "After Decoding: What?" Carol Chomsky (1976) had struggling readers whose reading progress had stalled read a text while simultaneously listening to a recording of the same text on a tape recorder. The readers were asked to read the assigned text in this way repeatedly until they reached a point at which they could read it independently and fluently. Then, students were assigned to read a new text in a similar fashion. Of course, this assisted practice led students to the point at which they could read the assigned passage well. More interesting was that progress was also detected on new passages that had never before been read by the students. In addition to gains in sheer reading achievement, Chomsky also noted improvements in students' attitude and confidence. They had reached a level of reading an assigned text that was just as good as that of a more proficient reader!

Though many books and other written texts can now be purchased with an accompanying recorded tape or disc, advances in digital technology have increased the potential for using technology-assisted reading for instruction. While Chomsky had to record her passages on an old-fashioned tape recorder, teachers (and students) today can create their own recorded versions of texts on their computers or mobile devices. Computer applications allow teachers to record their own reading of a text as a podcast or even video (with audio). When teachers use these applications, they will have an electronic file of the recording. Teachers no longer need to feel hamstrung by physical cassette tapes or discs that can be lost or damaged; they can have all of their files saved in one location or they can share the files to multiple locations with the click of a mouse. In fact, these digital recordings can be transported electronically to students in other locations for their families, other teachers, or even pen pals to read and hear.

Captioned Television

One of the more unusual forms of assisted reading that has been around for decades is captioned television. When viewers watch a captioned television (or recorded video) program with the sound volume turned up, they are essentially engaging in a form of assisted reading—the viewer sees the words on the television screen and hears the words being read at the same (or nearly the same) time.

Thus, watching captioned television has the potential for improving reading. Indeed, in his book *The Read-Aloud Handbook*, Jim Trelease (2006) claims that one of the reasons for Finland's remarkable success in literacy has been the wide employment of captioned television with young students. Certainly, in a 30-minute television program, a viewer will encounter several words; this, along with the volume being on, provides viewers with oral support while reading those words on their own.

Recently, we received a note from a colleague, Donna Pelikan, who told us about a teacher's interaction with the parent of a struggling reader:

> The teacher asked the mother of a struggling reader to find 10 to 20 minutes per day to read to her son. The mom commented that she didn't have much time due to her job. After a few months, though, the little guy really became a very good reader, so the teacher called the mom to praise her and ask what she was doing. Well, the mom said that her son was accompanying her to the Joe Clark Bar and Grill where she worked several nights a week. He was singing along with the karaoke machine each time.

Sometimes assisted reading can show up in some of the most unusual places!

READING PRACTICE

To become fluent at any endeavor, one needs to practice. Think of how much practice you had to put into driving a car before driving became a fairly automatic task. If you are good at a particular sport, think of all the practice you put into your golf swing or jump shot before it became second nature. The same is true in reading. The old cliché "the more you read, the better reader you will become" has much truth to it. Let's explore how students can develop as fluent and proficient readers through practice.

Wide Reading

Perhaps the most common form of reading practice occurs when a reader reads a text once and then moves on to read a new text.

This—essentially one text after another—is called wide reading and it is the type of reading most people, adults as well as children, do.

Most adults will finish a book and then move on to a totally new book or the next book in a series. Similarly, when adults pick up the daily newspaper, they may move topically from the national news, to the local news, to the sports, to the comics and the advice columns; then, tomorrow, they will engage in a similar routine but with tomorrow's newspaper.

This routine sounds similar to what happens in classrooms across the country. Students read a story or chapter from a text book, talk about it with the teacher and classmates, do some follow-up extension activities, and perhaps take a quiz over the content of the passage. Then, the next day, they will follow a similar routine with a new story or chapter. Clearly, this form of wide reading forms the heart of most instructional reading programs.

Although this routine is common practice, wide reading can also be done in other ways. Independent reading at school, often called Sustained Silent Reading, is a form of wide reading. Every day, teachers give students 10–15 minutes to read on their own a text of their own choosing; the following day, they continue reading from where they left off the day before. Reutzel, Jones, Fawson, and Smith (2008) argue that independent wide reading can work best when students are provided with guidance and made accountable for the time spent reading. Thus, by providing students with this type of reading and some follow-up activity, students will improve their fluency skills.

Wide reading can also occur at home. Rasinski, Padak, and Fawcett (2009) describe a schoolwide program where students are challenged to read 20 or more minutes at home. Done over the course of a school year, the cumulative number of minutes is a million or more, an impressive figure to say the least. Several schools have embraced the activity and have seen reading achievement and students' motivation to read increase. A similar wide reading program—summer reading— can also be designed for the summer months, when children often regress in their reading development. A growing body of scholarship (e.g., Morgan, Mraz, Padak, & Rasinski, 2008; Stanovich, 1986) and research (e.g., Allington et al., 2010) suggests that if teachers increase the amount of students' independent and wide reading, it will yield improvements in students' reading fluency and other measures of reading proficiency.

Deep and Repeated Reading

Sometimes one reading is simply not enough, especially when working with students who are struggling in reading or who are asked to read a text that is challenging or written above their own reading levels. These students may need to read a text two, three, or even more times. This form of reading practice has been called repeated reading (Samuels, 1979); we also like the term *deep reading*, as it suggests that good reading practice, like a mighty river, is both wide and deep. (This term/definition also suggests that with every rereading of a text, the reader is able to get to a deeper level of proficiency and meaning.)

In a study of struggling readers, Samuels (1979) found that having students practice reading a text several times until they achieved a level of mastery on the text resulted not only in improvements on the texts that they practice but also in a carryover effect, whereby improvements were noted when students started on a new text they had not seen before. Since this initial report, there have been a number of studies on repeated reading. A recent critical review of this research (Rasinski, Reutzel, Chard, & Linan-Thompson, 2011) concludes that repeated or deep reading is an effective instructional practice for improving reading fluency (and other reading competencies) among students at a variety of levels of development using texts of varying level and type.

Although the concept of repeated reading is well established, there are some scholars and teachers who worry about its implementation. Because fluency and progress in fluency is often measured in terms of reading speed, repeated reading practice has often been implemented with a goal of achieving a certain reading speed. When the goal of reading instruction is speed, the reader's focus shifts from making meaning to reading fast. We think the reasons for doing repeated reading need further consideration, which we will do in the next chapter on the art of teaching fluency.

READING IN PHRASES

Ultimately, teachers can look for some key and observable behaviors to determine how their students are reading. First, good readers read in phrases—noun phrases, verb phrases, and prepositional phrases, whereas readers who struggle with reading tend to read in more of a word-by-word manner. Although a focus on phrased reading does not get much attention in school reading programs, teachers should include it as an essential focus for proficient reading in each fluency program. Helping students learn how to read in phrases should help their ability to read in phrases. For example, consider the following sentence:

Woman without her man is nothing!

When most individuals read this as a continuous sentence, they assume the author is being sexist. But, what if one were to read the same words again and, this time, add slight pauses where we have placed slash marks?

Woman/ without her/ man is nothing! (Woman: without her, man is nothing!)

One will notice that the meaning has changed considerably—not by changing the words or the word order, but simply by phrasing the text in a slightly different way.

Good phrasing in reading is important because it can help facilitate meaning; of course, lack of phrasing is likely to hinder meaning. As teachers, you might have heard students read in an excessively slow, word-by-word, staccato-like manner. Hopefully, by giving the student clues to phrasing, the teacher can help students with what might be a slow, painful process. For example, certain words in English, particularly prepositions, noun markers, and function words, have limited meaning when they are considered alone but can be "clue" words to help students create meaningful phrases when they read. The word *if*, for example, has very little meaning by itself; but, put it into a syntactically appropriate phrase and sentence—*If you decide to go, be sure to wear a jacket*—and that single word is critical to the meaning the author wishes to convey.

We hope you think phrasing is important, but you're probably wondering how you could teach and nurture it in your students. Though we certainly need more data reports from teachers who are teaching phrasing and scholars who are researching phrasing, we'd still like to offer a few suggestions for teaching phrasing in the classroom.

To begin, many teachers start by using word walls, displays of charts that contain words in their classrooms. Word walls provide teachers and students the opportunity to read the words on the classroom word wall and add new words to the classroom word wall regularly. Our one concern about word walls is that by putting the words in isolation, we may be sending a message to students that reading words in a word-by-word manner, whether on a word wall or in connected written discourse, is appropriate.

To help combat word-by-word reading, the teacher, and students, could add a "phrase place" to their word wall. This way, as new words are added to the word wall, students can add phrases or short sentences containing the targeted words to the "phrase place," too. So, for example, as the words *sister, brother, vase, dog,* and *pet* are added to the word wall, the following phrases and sentences are added to the phrase place: *My big sister, her little brother, the broken vase, my dog Ginger, Pet the dog, The dog broke the vase.* Teachers and students could take a few minutes each day to chorally read both the set of words and phrases. By practicing the phrases, students not only get additional practice with the targeted words, but they can practice the words in the context of syntactically appropriate chunks for phrases, too.

In addition to adding adjective phrases, the teacher can use the phrase place for a number of other variations. The phrase place could also contain phrases made noteworthy by famous people or documents from the past. Imagine having these phrases on your phrase place:

- I have a dream . . .
- My fellow Americans . . .
- We the people . . .
- Four score and seven years ago . . .
- Government of the people . . .
- When in the course of human events . . .
- The only thing we have to fear . . .

In Figures 4.1 and 4.2, we list common English proverbs and idioms (often-used meaningful phrases and sentences) that students would have fun practicing, learning, and using in their own oral and written language. Besides developing an understanding of these important expressions, it would give students the opportunity to practice the art of phrased reading.

Figure 4.1. Common Proverbs

Absence makes the heart grow fonder.
Actions speak louder than words.
After the feast comes the reckoning.
All that glitters is not gold.
An apple a day keeps the doctor away.
The apple doesn't fall far from the tree.
Bad news travels fast.
Barking dogs seldom bite.
Beauty is in the eyes of the beholder.
Beggars can't be choosers.
The best things in life are free.
Better a live coward than a dead hero.
Better late than never.
Better safe than sorry.
The bigger they are, the harder they fall.
A bird in the hand is worth two in the bush.
Birds of a feather flock together.
Blood is thicker than water.
Charity begins at home.
Clothes do not make the man.
Curiosity killed the cat.
Do as I say, not as I do.
Don't bite off more than you can chew.
Don't bite the hand that feeds you.
Don't count your chickens before they're hatched.
Don't cry over spilled milk.
Don't judge a book by its cover.
Don't judge a man until you've walked in his boots.
Don't look a gift horse in the mouth.
Don't put all your eggs in one basket.
Don't put off for tomorrow what you can do today.
Don't put the cart before the horse.
Familiarity breeds contempt.
The first step is always the hardest.
A fool and his money are soon parted.
Forewarned is forearmed.
A friend in need is a friend indeed.
A friend who shares is a friend who cares.
Good things come in small packages.
The grass is always greener on the other side of the fence.
Haste makes waste.
He who hesitates is lost.

He who laughs last, laughs best.
Hindsight is better than foresight.
If at first you don't succeed, try, try again.
If you can't beat them, join them.
If you can't stand the heat, get out of the kitchen.
Imitation is the sincerest form of flattery.
In unity there is strength.
It never rains but it pours.
It takes two to tango.
Leave well enough alone.
A leopard cannot change its spots.
Lightning never strikes twice in the same place.
Look before you leap.
Love is blind.
Love makes the world go round.
Make hay while the sun shines.
Man does not live by bread alone.
A man is known by the company he keeps.
Might makes right.
Misery loves company.
A miss is as good as a mile.
Money does not grow on trees.
Necessity is the mother of invention.
No news is good news.
No pain, no gain.
Nothing hurts like the truth.
Nothing ventured, nothing gained.
Old habits die hard.
One good turn deserves another.
One man's gravy is another man's poison.
One swallow does not a summer make.
The pen is mightier than the sword.
Possession is nine-tenths of the law.
Practice makes perfect.
The proof of the pudding is in the eating.
The road to hell is paved with good intentions.
Rome wasn't built in a day.
The spirit is willing, but the flesh is weak.
The squeaking wheel gets the oil.
Strike while the iron is hot.
There is no honor among thieves.
There's more than one way to skin a cat.
There's no fool like an old fool.
There's no place like home.

Figure 4.1. Common Proverbs *(continued)*

Too many chiefs, not enough Indians.
Too many cooks spoil the broth.
Two heads are better than one.
Two's company, but three's a crowd.
Variety is the spice of life.
The way to a man's heart is through his stomach.
When in Rome, do as the Romans do.
When the cat's away, the mice play.
Where there's smoke, there's fire.
You can lead a horse to water, but you can't make him drink.
You can't have your cake and eat it too.
You can't teach an old dog new tricks.
You have to take the good with the bad.
You reap what you sow.
You're never too old to learn.

Figure 4.2. Common Idioms

Actions speak louder than words.
  People's intentions can be judged better by what they do, than by what
  they say.
Add insult to injury.
  Further a loss with mockery or indignity; worsen an unfavorable situation
An arm and a leg
  Very expensive or costly; a large amount of money
At the drop of a hat
  Without any hesitation; instantly
Back to the drawing board
  When an attempt fails and it's time to start all over
The ball is in your court.
  It is up to you to make the next decision or take the next step
Barking up the wrong tree
  Looking in the wrong place; accusing the wrong person
Be glad to see the back of (someone)
  Be happy when a person leaves
Beating around the bush
  Avoiding the main topic; not speaking directly about the issue
Best of both worlds
  All the advantages
Best thing since sliced bread
  A good invention or innovation; a good idea or plan

Bite off more than you can chew
  Take on a task that is way too big
Blessing in disguise
  Something good that isn't recognized at first
Burn the midnight oil
  Work late into the night, alluding to the time before electric lighting
Can't judge a book by its cover
  Cannot judge something primarily on appearance
Caught between two stools
  Having difficultly choosing between two alternatives
Costs an arm and a leg
  Is very expensive
Cross that bridge when you come to it
  Deal with a problem if and when it becomes necessary, not before
Cry over spilled milk
  Complain about a problem from the past
Curiosity killed the cat.
  Being inquisitive can lead you into an unpleasant situation.
Cut corners
  Do something badly to save money
Cut the mustard
  Succeed; come up to expectations; be adequate enough to compete or
  participate
Devil's advocate
  Person who presents a counterargument
Don't count your chickens before the eggs have hatched.
  Don't make plans for something that might not happen.
Don't give up your day job.
  You are not very good at something. You could definitely not do it
  professionally.
Don't put all your eggs in one basket.
  Do not put all your resources in one possibility.
Drastic times call for drastic measures.
  When you are extremely desperate, you need to take drastic actions.
Elvis has left the building.
  The show has come to an end. It's all over.
Every cloud has a silver lining.
  Be optimistic; even difficult times will lead to better days.
Far cry from
  Very different from

Figure 4.2. Common Idioms *(continued)*

Feel a bit under the weather
  Feel slightly ill
Give the benefit of the doubt
  Believe someone's statement without needing proof
Hear it through the grapevine
  Hear rumors about something or someone
Hit the nail on the head
  Do or say something exactly right
Hit the sack/sheets/hay
  Go to bed
A hot potato
  An issue (mostly current) about which many people are talking and which
  is usually disputed
In the heat of the moment
  Spontaneously in reaction to something
Jump on the bandwagon
  Join a popular trend or activity
Keep something at bay
  Keep something away
Kill two birds with one stone
  Accomplish two different tasks at the same time
Last straw
  The last in a series of grievances that makes a situation unbearable
Let sleeping dogs lie.
  Do not disturb a situation as it is, since it would result in trouble or
  complications.
Let the cat out of the bag
  Share information that was previously concealed
Make a long story short
  Come to the point; leave out details
Method to my madness
  Plan behind my seemingly random or unusual behavior
Miss the boat
  Miss an opportunity or chance
Not a spark of decency
  No manners
Not playing with a full deck
  Lacking intelligence or common sense

Off one's rocker
  Crazy, demented, out of one's mind, in a confused or befuddled state of
  mind, senile
On the ball
  Understanding the situation well
Once in a blue moon
  Happening very rarely
A penny for your thoughts
  A way of asking what someone is thinking
A picture is worth a thousand words.
  A visual presentation is far more descriptive than words.
Piece of cake
  Easy or simple
Pull the wool over someone's eyes
  Deceive someone in order to prevent them from knowing something
See eye to eye
  Agree on something
Sit on the fence
  Not make a decision
Speak of the devil!
  We were just talking about you and here you are!
Steal someone's thunder
  Use someone else's idea for personal gain
Take with a grain of salt
  Not take what someone says too seriously
A taste of your own medicine
  A dose of what you have done to others
Straight from the horse's mouth
  From the authoritative source
Whole nine yards
  Everything; all of it
Wouldn't be caught dead (doing)
  Would never do
Your guess is as good as mine.
  I have no idea; I do not know the answer.

Another adaptation of the "phrase place" is to alter the way the words are presented to students. Students could have their own individual phrase places in a personal folder that they could practice individually. For example, the students could work at the phrase place in a classroom center, where students are required to spend some time doing classroom-related activities. Or, each day, the teacher could upload the phrases into a PowerPoint presentation and then flash the phrases to students in a different order and at increasing speeds.

Another approach to teaching phrasing is to physically mark phrase boundaries for students within texts. Many phrase boundaries / are marked / for readers / by punctuation (periods, commas, semi-colons, and so forth). // Other phrase boundaries / are not marked at all; //they need to be inferred / by the reader. // And / if the reader / is already reading in a word-by-word manner, // it may be difficult for him or her / to infer or predict / where those boundaries may be. // For those word-by-word readers, / actually marking the text / to show phrase boundaries / could help / to facilitate / more fluent reading.//

We have illustrated / how such markings / might look in the previous and current paragraphs. // Normally when we do this / with our students, / we simply take a pencil / and mark / the boundaries / with single and double slash marks. // Although we may not agree / 100% of the time / on the appropriate placement / of the phrase boundaries, / we are much more likely / to agree / in where we locate them / than we are to disagree.// Many speech and acting teachers use a similar coding system to assist their students in reading/performing their texts with appropriate phrasing and meaning.

Granted, having students read with slash marks embedded in the text may not be the most authentic reading experience. However, teachers can use this activity to help students combine these phrase texts with repeated readings to create an instructional scenario that combines two forms of fluency instruction. Students could read a text marked with phrase boundaries several times. Then, on the following day or days, students could be asked to read the same text a few more times without the phrase markings. Students would have to infer the phrase boundaries from their previous reading and apply that knowledge to reading the unmarked text. If the teacher integrates more than one element of effective instruction seamlessly into a lesson, the students' gain will be more than the sum of the lesson parts. Each part can influence and expand the impact of the others.

Much of the research on helping to develop proficiency in phrasing occurred in previous decades. However, several studies that have been conducted point to great potential for moving students out of the all too common word-by-word reading to more productive and meaningful fluent reading.

FLUENCY AND COMPLEX TEXTS

One of the more controversial recommendations found in the Common Core State Standards is the expectation that students should be reading material that is considerably more challenging than what has been norm in previous years. We can understand the reasoning behind such a recommendation. If we want students to increase and accelerate their reading proficiency beyond what they had previously been achieving, students will have to successfully read texts that are more complex and more challenging than those read by students of previous generations. In a similar fashion, musicians and athletes continually increase the challenge of their tasks in order to accelerate the development of their particular skills. We can also, however, understand the concern raised by thoughtful literacy educators across the country. If many students are highly challenged by the texts they are currently asked to read and understand, won't giving students even more-challenging and more-complex texts lead to frustration and an eventual loss of desire for reading?

How can we help students negotiate these more complex and more challenging texts that they will be encountering? The answer is in reading fluency. The instructional tools we have outlined in this chapter will provide the scaffolded support for students to handle more-difficult reading materials. Substantive reading support can be provided using the following fluency approaches: reading a text to students and building their knowledge background for the topic prior to having students read it on their own (model reading), having students read a text while simultaneously listening to a more fluent reading of the text by another reader(s) (assisted reading), and having students read a text more than once, each time for a different and authentic purpose (repeated reading). I think we can all recall occasions when we have been challenged to read something that was, on the surface, more difficult than what we had generally read. Yet, through the same scaffolds we were able to successfully and meaningfully master that text.

A study on reading fluency by Stahl and Heubach (2005) sheds some light on the issue of text complexity and fluency. A fluency instructional routine incorporating several of the elements mentioned in this chapter was implemented over the course of a school year in 14 classrooms. Not surprisingly, students given the fluency instruction made significant gains in their reading achievement over the course of the year—indeed, all but two of the 125 students made significantly greater than expected growth in reading achievement. What *was* surprising was that the students who seemed to gain the greatest benefits did so when they were reading texts that were generally more difficult than the texts they normally encountered. The authors explain that the additional support provided by the fluency program allowed students to be successful with more challenging texts and thus accelerate their reading progress beyond normal expectations. Certainly, more research in this area is called for. However, as challenging students with increasingly more-complex texts becomes commonplace in our classrooms, the fluency instruction tools presented in this chapter offer reasonable ways for helping teachers help students deal with this new reality.

CLOSING COMMENTS

In order to teach and nurture fluent reading, we have several tools at hand. These tools include reading to students, assisted reading, wide reading, deep reading, and helping students phrase text appropriately and meaningfully. These elements are what we call the science of teaching reading fluency—that is, there is a fair amount of research, theory, and scholarly writing that supports using these elements instructionally with students. But, as most teachers realize, good teaching is both scientific and artful. In the next chapter, we will explore how we can move fluency from the mechanistic instruction that students often find less engaging to the more authentic and artful approaches to fluency that use these scientific approaches with a number of different types of texts.

THINK ABOUT IT

To what extent do you see instructional fluency activities being used in your school? Do you regularly see choral reading? Is repeated reading something that is commonly used in your classroom or other classrooms in your school? Do you view teachers in your school valuing these types of activities?

WHAT WE THINK

We are seeing, more and more, teachers incorporating the activities described in this chapter into their own teaching. However, we often see these activities being done for purposes other than reading. For example, choral reading is often employed as a way to start the school day. And repeated reading is often employed as a way to get students to read faster. We think these activities need to be incorporated into focused instruction on authentic reading fluency—fluency that is marked by increased automaticity in word recognition and improved prosody or expression. Once fluency instruction becomes an intentional part of each classroom day, teachers should see an improvement in reading fluency and reading comprehension among all students, but especially among those students who struggle in becoming fluent readers.

CHAPTER 5

Fluency as Art

In recent iterations of fluency instruction, fluency has been taught, for the most part, as a science. That is to say, when fluency instruction takes place, it is usually focused on increasing a scientific measure of reading fluency—oral reading rate. Growth in fluency is measured by gains in reading rate or speed. Research on repeated reading had students reading the same passage up to 15 times (Herman, 1985; Samuels, 1979) before moving on to another passage. Though this might work for ideal, cooperative students, most students who need help with fluency or dislike reading, will not enjoy such reading experiences. For these students, it is tough enough to get them to read something once, let alone up to 15 times. Telling them to read the same thing another 14 times may seem like cruel and unusual punishment.

Thus, initial attempts to employ repeated reading as a classroom intervention were often met with only limited success. Students did not readily see the reason for having to read the same text over and over. Borrowing from connectionism (Thorndike, 1898) and behavioral conditioning theory (Skinner, 1954), teachers began using materials that allowed students to monitor their own progress and offered rewards and praise for increases in rate. The rationale was that if the students knew how much good it was doing them, they would be motivated to complete the required reading. For example, some teachers still use one popular fluency intervention program, which requires students to chart their initial reading rate in words-per-minute with a blue pencil and then again after 10 repetitions with a red pencil. After the students finish the progressively complex text at a given level, they proceed up a step.

Unfortunately, this style of fluency instruction is not necessarily correlated to general reading achievement. After several readings, students quickly concluded that the best way to gain kudos was to read as fast as they could. Once they read the passage quickly, they would answer literal comprehension questions at the end of the passage and then race along to the next level. Additionally, because the repeated readings were done silently, many students discovered that they could skip most of the multiple readings and still show improvement quickly, especially when they made a concerted effort to read faster. The result of this approach is students who were increasing their reading rates but often at the expense of comprehension.

To be fair, this approach to fluency as a science has its strengths. When enacted as prescribed, it has the backing of research, is instantly quantifiable, and, in some cases, results in improved reading achievements. Yet, as we have mentioned previously, one drawback with this scientifically oriented approach is that students begin to believe speed is the primary reading goal. Moreover, the struggling readers, who need the most assistance from fluency instruction, often don't remain sufficiently committed to repeated reading. Thus, the teacher is still challenged with finding a strategy to get students engaged enough in each passage to truly build fluency. Plus, they must find a method for the students who are engaged to get them to slow down enough to understand what they were reading. And then, a solution came from an unlikely source.

IN TUNE

A colleague of ours told us he used to sing in a choir. He said:

> We often practiced until we were blue in the face—not really, but you get the idea. We didn't mind that much because we knew people were going to be listening to us and we wanted to sound our best. The teacher in me saw that I also sometimes learned vocabulary when we practiced new songs, and this got me to thinking about when I had been in a play, and I started to see the similarities. When you rehearse for a play, you are assigned a part, given a script, and read through it to find out what it's about. If there are words you don't know, you look them up or ask someone, because you can't really say your lines if you don't know what they mean. You read the script again to focus more on your own lines, and probably another dozen times to commit your lines to memory. And like singing in the choir, you rehearse because you want to do your best in front of the audience. I was starting to think both these things might be good ways to get kids to improve their reading skills.

It turns out he wasn't alone in his epiphany. A few progressive teachers reasoned that by taking songs into the classroom, particularly familiar songs with unfamiliar verses, students would be practicing repeated reading as they learned how to sing the song. Others took the idea a step further, by using poetry and having the students all read aloud at the same time. They found this allowed shy and timid students a chance to practice oral reading without being singled out.

Poetry is indeed an engaging and artful way to build fluency. For readers who have caught the performance bug, reading poetry can be the ideal outlet for individual expression. Although reading poetry is generally a solo activity, there are several excellent books with poems for two voices. One we especially like is Paul Fleischman's *Joyful Noise*, a collection of poems about insects beautifully laid out for two people or small groups to perform. Additionally, many poems and famous speeches can be easily adapted into Readers Theatre. Teachers can use this to teach social studies and build fluency at the same time!

Indeed, Readers Theatre has been one of the most powerful and effective implementations of repeated reading. A form of theater that involves minimal props and movement, Readers Theatre can be easily implemented in any classroom or subject area. Students are given a script and assigned a part at the beginning of the week and are provided with 10–15 minutes of class time to rehearse over the next few days. Then, at the end of the unit or week, there is a performance, and family members are invited to attend. (We have found that when kids know they are going to perform, their degree of engagement increases exponentially.)

Readers Theatre is the logical next step in a classroom that has done some choral reading. It allows readers to take the stage, one line at a time, to perform text either individually, in tandem, in groups, or in unison, depending on the script. Teachers found that employing a script, assigning parts, and having the students read their lines standing shoulder to shoulder was something they could do right in the classroom. Because there are few physical movements in Readers Theatre, all the acting or portrayal of meaning has to be done through the voice. This is the perfect venue for developing that most underappreciated aspect of fluency—prosody. Perhaps even better, because they know they will be performing for an audience, students involved in Readers Theatre and similar activities actually want to rehearse.

AN IMPETUS FOR REHEARSAL

Repetition as a means of building fluency is certainly not a new concept in the arts. Although not referred to in the same terms, musicians increase their fluency, or ability to play at the appropriate pace and expression, by practicing the same piece over and over. The reason they do so is no mystery. As one violinist explained, because "I'm going to be playing this in public next week, there are certain expectations of me and I don't want to make any mistakes in front of an audience." We've found that, like the violinist, children who know they are going to be performing for their peers, parents, teachers, and others have a similar outlook. One 3rd-grader, Kuanli, said, "I know it's important that we all do our best reading so everyone will think we're the bomb!" The students want to be successful, so they take the initiative to practice for their audience.

THINK ABOUT IT

Can you remember the first time you knew someone was going to listen to you sing, or play a musical instrument, or see you in a play? What were your own feelings leading up to the big day? How did you feel afterward? Contrast that with how you might have felt if you were called on in class to read something with which you were unfamiliar. Were you a good "cold reader," or were you one of the many children who felt exposed at having to perform on the spot with no rehearsal?

WHAT WE THINK

Even if you have fond memories of being called on in class to read an unfamiliar passage aloud, chances are you were nervous the first time you performed in or before a live audience. Whether you were going to be playing in a recital, acting in a skit, or reading a poem in front of the class, you wanted to be sure you did not mess up by forgetting your lines, playing the wrong notes, or stumbling over difficult words. Chances are that you taxed the patience of your parents, siblings, and friends by having them consistently listen to you rehearse. Now, think back on how many times you went over whatever it was that you were going to perform to help ensure that the worst situation didn't happen to you. The same practice that gave you the confidence to perform also served to increase your fluency. The growth that resulted from rehearsing a musical instrument made you a better musician overall. The ease with which you performed the speech you rehearsed was reflected in the next new thing you read. Regardless of the medium, you became better through practice.

THE ART OF FLUENCY INSTRUCTION

By thinking of fluency instruction as performance, we move it into the realm of art. Texts that include poetry, songs, famous speeches, and scripts adapted from content-area subjects expand our notions of how we teach. Perhaps the best way to view fluency artfully is to see it in action. In what follows, we share vignettes of teachers using these types of texts and pushing the boundaries of fluency instruction and offer opportunities for you to bring it into your classroom.

Singing to Fluency

Our first stop is in 2nd-grade teacher Nellie Behling's (all names are pseudonyms) Kansas classroom, where Louis Armstrong's version of "What a Wonderful World" fills the air. It's fluency-building time, but the students don't know that. To them, it's a period of the day when they get to sing along to music. As Satchmo sings, Ms. Behling is passing out the binders that contain lyric sheets with numbered lines in page protectors. The students know from experience that they listen to the song once first and then the second time they sing along, tracing the words with their fingers. After the third time, she divides the class in half by birthdays—January through June on one side, July through December on another. Then, she begins her instruction by asking them to sing antiphonally–that is, the first group singing the odd-numbered lines and the second group singing the even-numbered lines. Later, she has them sing by gender, then by eye color. In each instance, she has the groups clustered together.

She told us she utilizes this grouping strategy because she knows that her reluctant singers/readers are more likely to respond when they are surrounded by other voices. We can see that the children obviously enjoy the activity. And, by the end of the singing, each student will have read the song at least 8 to 10 times. She said, "I started this last year after attending a reading conference where someone was talking about doing this for students learning English as a second language, but I thought, 'That would work in my class!' So I started doing it the last 15 minutes of class on Tuesdays and Thursdays. I give 3-minute reading assessments several times during the year, and I found everyone's fluency increasing beyond expectations, but by far the greatest gains were with the students who had been struggling the most." Ms. Behling went on to tell us that every Monday morning some of the kids ask her which songs they get to sing this week. She said she tries to introduce a new song every week and occasionally allows requests for favorite songs they've already done if time allows.

Your Turn

Here are the steps to follow to get started singing in your classroom.

1. First, choose the music. You'll want songs with a rich vocabulary appropriate for your class. You will also want songs that have a good balance of chorus and lyrical stanzas. This provides additional repeated reading. It is best to start with songs that have a slow to moderate tempo with clear phrasing.

Besides "What a Wonderful World" by Louis Armstrong, we would also encourage you to try one of the following:

"Take Me Out to the Ballgame"
"We Shall Overcome"
"Shenandoah"

Additionally, the Internet offers several great song resources. We found the following sites to be particularly helpful:

- www.theteachersguide.com/ChildrensSongs.htm
- www.niehs.nih.gov/kids/music.htm
- www.songsforteaching.com
- www.contemplator.com/america/
- www.scoutsongs.com/categories/patriotic.html

2. Introduce the song. The teacher should begin by having the class read through the lyrics together. Then, the teacher should play the music, so the students can enjoy the musicality of the song. To help give context to the song, the teacher might even tell a story or history about the song. Then, the teacher could play the song again, but, this time, everyone should read and/or sing along. The lyrics can also be marked up to cue students to appropriate phrasing when singing and reading. Note: To avoid memorization, rotate songs frequently. The point is for the students to be *reading*, rather than *reciting*.

3. Rinse and repeat. Or at least repeat. And think of the potential learning enhancements by taking advantage of using the lyrics as text. Doing rhyme hunts, finding synonyms for particularly interesting words, and identifying word families are all great opportunities for building word knowledge.

4. Keep it real. Take advantage of the seasons, holidays, and other events in children's lives to guide song selections. In addition, teachers can use songs to introduce or reinforce subject matter(s). Studying the American Revolution? A perfect time to sing "Yankee Doodle." In science or mathematics, teachers or students could create parodies to popular songs in which they embed important content that students are required to learn. The final determinant should be that the students enjoy the songs they are singing.

5. Give them a reason. Finally, find an audience for your readers/singers. It could be parents, an administrator, or other students. Allow them to show their newfound knowledge and abilities to another classroom. The teacher could even project lyrics on the Smart Board, PowerPoint, or overhead projector, so the audience can read along as the students sing and read. This way, not only does the audience become more "fluent," but they will also get an idea of what has been accomplished and what they can look forward to when they move into this class. Most important, the students will be more engaged throughout the singing process, knowing they will be performing in public.

THINK ABOUT IT

You may be asking yourself, that all sounds well and good but is there any evidence that singing actually increases fluency and helps with reading? Does this really work?

WHAT WE THINK

Does it work? In a word, absolutely. For example, a study of struggling 2nd-grade students found that the regular repeated singing and reading of songs over a 9-week period resulted in a nearly 7-month average gain in fluency. Best of all, as shown in Figure 5.1, a follow-up assessment showed continued accelerated growth (Biggs, Homan, Dedrick, Minick, & Rasinski, 2008).

Figure 5.1. Changes in Grade-Level Reading Achievement

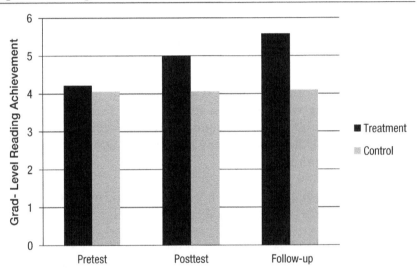

PERFORMING SCRIPTS

Next, we traveled to a school in the foothills of the Cascade Mountains in Washington. Our next teacher, Sully Johnson, has found that the pull-out students in his literacy intervention setting weren't responding to the phonics-based direct instruction he was taught in his recently completed master's special education program. As a one-time theater major, something he'd read in his master's program about Readers Theatre had caught his eye and came back to him.

He went online, found a site with free scripts, and downloaded one that looked interesting. His group consists of four 4th-grade boys all reading between a year and half and 2 years below grade-level reading norms. Sully noted:

> I chose a short script called *The Three Billy Goats Gruff*. I liked it because it seemed tailor-made for this group. It had the right number of parts and offered opportunities for the boys to show off a little. Surprisingly, the boys weren't familiar with the story.

Sully explained how the troll is a monster who lives under a bridge that three billy goat brothers have to cross in order to get to the "green, green grass of the other side." As he described parts to the boys, he could see the lights go on in one of the boy's eyes when he got to the part about the troll. Achilles was a 10-year-old, who had missed a lot of school his first 2 years because of a congenital medical problem. He was in Sully's class because he was reading at an early 2nd-grade level. He was smaller than most of the students in the class and was a born entertainer with great comic timing. Although Achilles's reading was the lowest in the group, from the first time Sully read the script, he knew immediately that Achilles should play the troll. The troll didn't have many lines, but he was full of bluff and bluster. Sully continued:

> I figured if Achilles could see how much fun he might have, he'd follow along to be sure he didn't miss his lines.

After a few minutes, Sully started what he called a "Model Echo Read Through (MERT)." He told the students he was going to read each line first, and then, if it was someone's part that was being read, that individual should read the line with him the second time and then read it the third time alone.

By doing this, Sully implemented a gradual release of responsibility as he was able to model reading with expression at the right pace and allow students to ease into saying their lines by themselves. Because the script was only a few pages long, it 'didn't take much time to read through it in this manner.

He followed this activity with the first solo reading. To get the students to start as a group, Sully alerted them to keep their eyes on him: "I tell them I will raise my head and that signals they should be ready. Then when I bring it down, they start."

Later, he said,

In total we ended up reading the script five times this first day and they got better with each reading. Everybody especially loved Achilles's troll and the part where the Big Billy Goat butts him off of the bridge. What was neat was seeing how much fun they all had!

Sully said younger students are sometimes afraid to read with volume or expression. As one student, Deshawn, explained, "We're not sure that it is okay to 'go a little crazy.'" To help them get into character, Sully modeled the difference between reading in a monotone, which the class called robot reading, and reading with expression, which they called reading like an actor. Sully said:

> There is a great trick I learned in the theater for bringing along kids who are either reading too quietly or without expression. Once you're sure that they aren't stumbling on the words, you take them aside and ask them to help you play a joke on the rest of the cast. You tell them, "Just for fun, read your lines twice as loud this time through. Overdo it! Exaggerate your lines! If your character is a little shy, try to make them even more shy. If your character is sort of mean, make them really mean. It they are just a little bit happy, make them wild with happiness."

When Sully got the desired results from the class, he reminded his students that this was exactly how the script should sound and that the audience was going to love it. To keep it fresh, he also reminded them that they would all get a chance to read any part they wanted in the next few days before they performed in front of the class on Friday. Interestingly, Achilles, who really latched on to the part of the blustering troll, was generally one of Sully's more reluctant readers. After the second session, he told Sully that he wanted to try reading the part of the Little Billy Goat Gruff on the following day. When he asked to take the script home to practice, Sully knew Achilles was hooked. And the next day, his rendition of the Little Billy Goat was spot-on funny.

By making Readers Theatre a regular and integral part of his reading curriculum, Sully found an artful opening for his students' reading. He reported, "Of course they love it. It's fun. But most importantly they are becoming better readers. Needless to say, everybody's fluency has increased. I give them the DRA (Developmental Reading

Assessment) twice a year and this year the latest test results showed that they'd made on the average over a year and a half's growth in 8 months. Achilles's classroom teacher came up to me in the hall in the middle of the year and asked what I had been doing with him. She told he'd actually volunteered to read aloud in class!"

Your Turn

Readers Theatre may be one of the simplest, most effective ways of improving fluency. What follows is a 5-day plan for bringing Readers Theatre into your classroom.

Choosing Scripts. As with songs, choose Readers Theatre scripts on the basis of seasonal themes, content-area study, or comedic value. The Internet offers a number of free download sites (see Figure 5.2).

The following 5-day format details how Readers Theatre can be implemented. Allow 20 minutes on Monday to introduce the script; 10 minutes each on Tuesday, Wednesday, and Thursday; and 10–15 minutes on Friday.

Monday: Introduce the script. This should take about 20 minutes. Use a mini-lesson to model a think-aloud aimed at a particular comprehension strategy, such as making connections, main ideas, or inferring word meanings. For younger and disfluent students, assign temporary parts and do a Model Echo Read Through (MERT). Scripts are sent home with the students to read through with an eye for choosing a part in which they are interested.

Figure 5.2. Website Sources for Readers Theatre Scripts and Information About Readers Theatre

www.aaronshep.com/rt
www.fictionteachers.com/classroomtheater/theater.html
www.busyteacherscafe.com/literacy/readers_theater.html
rtscripts.weebly.com/index.html
www.superteacherworksheets.com/readers-theater.html
www.teachingheart.net/readerstheater.htm
www.thebestclass.org/rtscripts.html
www.timelessteacherstuff.com
www.timrasinski.com
www.vtaide.com/png/theatre.htm

Tuesday: 10 minutes. Assign parts based on student preference. Conflicts can usually be resolved through rock/paper/scissors. Guide the students through highlighting their lines. Once finished, do the first read through. Students take the scripts home to practice their parts.

Wednesday: 10 minutes. On this day have the students practice their lines individually by whisper-reading. As they read, continue to navigate the room to discern if students have any difficulties with word recognition, meaning, and expression.

Thursday: 10 minutes. This is dress rehearsal day. The students get one last chance to rehearse as a group and prep for tomorrow's performance.

Friday: It's show time! Arrange an audience of parents, administrators, or peers. Create a stage: the classroom, the cafeteria, or the auditorium. Keep it simple, keep it fun, and don't forget to teach your students to bow during the applause!

This was the general format that Sully employed in this classroom. Over the course of the next year, Sully's students performed 23 Readers Theatre scripts. Although the goal of Readers Theatre is smooth, expressive reading, his students made double the expected gains in oral reading rate and showed significant growth in measure of word recognition and prosody. Additionally, scores on the districts' informal reading inventory were well above the end-of-the-year benchmark.

COMIC BOOK FLUENCY

Among struggling readers, engagement is a real concern. As indicated above, effective fluency instruction won't take place without student buy-in, so the teacher will need to incorporate it into the lesson in an "artistic" manner. For example, Ms. Vierney artistically created a solution for a reluctant 11-year-old reader who had fluency problems. Reyna, a Title I student in Ms. Vierney's 5th-grade class, exhibited a general disinterest in reading, but she loved talking about comic book characters. In fact, Ms. V said she remembered the light in Reyna's eyes when Reyna would talk about the X-Men comic book character Storm.

To help bring a personal connection to Reyna's reading, Ms. Vierney asked if Reyna could get two friends to help her create a class comic book based on female superheroes after school. She explained that they were looking for a comic book story about a character who went on an adventure. The next day, Reyna arrived with her two friends, Dana and Jess. Ms. V constructed a simple graphic organizer to get them started on the plot outline: adventure, conflict, resolution/solution (see Figure 5.3). She explained that the first thing they needed to do was jot down a storyline. She walked them through the organizer and let them decide what the problem was going to be, who was best to solve it (because of their super powers, and why), and how it would end. After writing out a plot outline, the students made rough sketches for the storyboard and filled in the story continuum box below the panels to describe what was happening.

Writing the characters and dialogue was next. Ms. V said she "reminded them that they would also have to brainstorm and think about what each super hero was going to say. Then, the next time we met, they started adding the word balloons. A couple of times the dialogue they choose was beyond their spelling ability, so I helped them out and made suggestions." Ms. V was surprised at the complexity of the language they came up with. "Then I picked up some superhero comic books and found the vocabulary load was really quite high. If I could get the girls to read comics and graphic novels by making them part of my reading instruction, so much the better!"

Figure 5.3. Ms. Vierney's Storyline Organizer Template

Drawing/Dialogue	Drawing/Dialogue	Drawing/Dialogue	Drawing/Dialogue
→ Description of Action →			
Drawing/Dialogue	Drawing/Dialogue	Drawing/Dialogue	Drawing/Dialogue
→ Description of Action →			

Once the storyline and dialogue were finished, Ms. V asked them—the authors—to read the comic books out loud. Although tentative, they agreed. Ms. V said she'd take pictures of the panels and put them into a PowerPoint presentation. That way, the rest of the class would be able to see the pictures, while Reyna and her friends read the dialogue.

Their first read through for Ms. V got them so excited about performing that they decided they would do their comic at the semiweekly class Read-A-Loud Display Café. The Read-A-Loud Café is a venue where the students in Ms. V's class routinely are given a 3-minute slot to share their favorite poem, passage, song lyric, or joke as a way to practice expressive reading. Because Reyna and her friends worked together, their 10-minute story fell within the time guidelines, so it was a perfect venue to share it with the class.

Best of all, in preparation for their performance, they willingly rehearsed the script multiple times, which increased their reading fluency. With guidance from Ms. V, Reyna and her friends not only overcame their initial reluctance to read aloud but, encouraged by the response of their peers, they asked to be able to create another script in the future.

Since then, Ms. V has created a monthly Graphic Novel Live (GNL) event. "I had no idea it would catch on like this," she said. "But the upshot is they are not only reading more, they are reading better! And I find that when they are writing their own scripts, they seek out more complex dialogue." She said she believes the repeated reading they do when rehearsing seems to be making a big difference in other areas as well."

GNL is now a classwide activity: "I've gone from having some of the kids write their own scripts to allowing anyone to perform existing books [comics and graphic novels], which is really the point." Because engagement has increased, she said her class is doing more outside reading, too. Ms. V says she can see a direct connection to the increase in her class's overall reading achievement—especially with her low readers.

Our school administers the Johns's Basic Reading Inventory (BRI) in September and May and although everyone is showing greater than expected growth, my bottom third is showing the most dramatic results. Several gained nearly 2 years' growth in 8 months. I personally think it is all the practice they put into performing on Graphic Novel Live!

And Reyna? Not only has her reading improved, but she's busy working on what she calls her third "graphic shorty." Not too surprisingly, Ms. Vierney tells us Reyna is now in the habit of reading them aloud to anyone who will listen. And, as Mrs. V had hoped, Reyna is now a fluent reader.

POETRY AND PERFORMANCE

Janet Ferguson has been approaching fluency instruction as a performing art for many years. Her path to using it in the classroom is an interesting one. In her early years in education, she told us:

> I've always loved reading out loud, and I couldn't understand why everybody wouldn't love it as well. When I was doing my student teaching, it dawned on me that for some people, reading out loud in front of people was the last thing they wanted to do, due to the fact that it was embarrassing for them because they didn't do it well.

She asked herself how she could get those children who were struggling over that hump of insecurity. It seemed simple with emergent readers, but she was doing her student teaching in a middle school, where the patterns of avoidance were already entrenched.

> I knew simple modeling wasn't going to be enough for a couple of reasons. To begin with, many of my students who didn't like to read were boys, and as a woman, I was afraid I was just reinforcing their bias that reading was a "girl thing."

So, with the permission of their cooperating teacher (who was also a woman), she said she gave the class an interest inventory. Many interest inventories are aimed at finding the reading interests of students, but because these kids currently weren't reading very much, she decided to try to find out what kept their attention and what texts might satisfy those interests. She used an inventory that moved beyond the usual "what do you like to read" questions to questions like "If you could be anyone in the world, who would that be?" and "What is the coolest thing you can think of doing?" to understand what interests drove these students.

Not surprisingly, she found that the boys were more interested in sports. If these boys engaged in any voluntary reading, they tended to gravitate to sports topics—sports biographies, recaps, and so on. So, with help of her husband—who, she says, "I don't think has ever missed a game of anything"—she found a short poem on baseball called "Baseball's Sad Lexicon" (sometimes also called "Tinker to Evers to Chance") by Franklin Pierce Adams about three players on the Chicago Cubs who specialized in double plays. "I had them do in antiphonally—you know, kinda like call and response. They had such fun with it that they wanted to do another. This time my husband suggested they might like 'Casey at the Bat' by Ernest Thayer."

"Baseball's Sad Lexicon" by Franklin Pierce Adams

These are the saddest of possible words:
"Tinker to Evers to Chance."
Trio of bear cubs, and fleeter than birds,
Tinker and Evers and Chance.
Ruthlessly pricking our gonfalon bubble,
Making a Giant hit into a double—
Words that are heavy with nothing but trouble:
"Tinker to Evers to Chance."

Published in the *New York Evening Mail*, July 10, 1910.

And he was right. Once the boys heard her perform it, he said they couldn't wait to start rehearsing. Because engagement for these three students was such an issue, this was big. When they performed it in class, it was a hit. "I can't tell you how much Sandy—I mean Ms. Ivey (the cooperating teacher)—and I were moved. These were boys who almost never willingly read aloud. And here they were—reading poetry, no less!"

After that experience, not only did the three boys want to do another poem, but much of the rest of the class thought it would be fun to do, too. The demand was great enough that the cooperating teacher decided to incorporate this fluency building activity into her monthly unit planning.

Today, Janet Ferguson has her own 7th-grade class. "Since I picked up in my master's how important fluency development is well into high school, I've made what I call 'Poetry Roundup' an integral part of my fluency instruction, too."

Poems are self-selected from her classroom library and several websites. Once she's okayed the poem, the kids do the rest. Parts are assigned and she allows 10–15 minutes of class time for rehearsal for the 3 days leading up to the reading, although she's seen the kids practicing outside of class when the Thursday afternoon performance is imminent.

> During our poetry unit, it's different of course. We use the poem as literary text and investigate the various facets that make it a good poem. But for Poetry Roundup, it's really all theirs. The gravy is the higher scores we are seeing in overall reading achievement, which seem to be the result of increases in fluency and, I believe, the extra exposure to some really great poetry!

On Roundup Day, as she calls it, she allows 15–20 minutes for performances and, like the growing number of teachers who use performance as an impetus for fluency practice, she optionally invites parents, administrators, and other classrooms to listen.

Janet's Tips for a Poetry Roundup Day:

Day 1: Plan ahead! Help them choose the poem. Point them in the direction of their interests. Then, show them how to divvy it up into parts, if they are working as a group. I suggest making copies and using highlighters. This can all be done in 15–20 minutes, depending of the size of your class. If you've never modeled good expressive reading for them, now's the time.

Day 2: Let them rehearse for 10–15 minutes. Circulate among the groups and individuals and help with pronunciation and understanding.

Day 3: Have them read the poems to one another. This can be done simultaneously. Encourage them to push the envelope on varying their pace, expression, and volume. Take some time and model hamming it up a bit. Allow 10–15 minutes or so.

Day 4: Poetry Roundup! This is the fun part! Turn your classroom into a performance café by turning the lights down a little and moving a couple desks to make a performance area. Allow 15–20 minutes. If we've had a good week, I serve popcorn. But you can do anything you want. The point is to make it special. Have fun!

One of the students, Bibi, explained that "at first I didn't know if I ever wanted to read a poem in front of people, but now I do. She lets us do some of the really weird and crazy ones and those are pretty cool."

ON STAGE

Fluency as art often means fluency as performance, and its association with theater is no accident. The connection between theatrical performance and reading is a curious one. Though theater and reading are usually thought of as two separate entities, students enrolled in a drama-based curriculum outperformed their peers in measures of reading comprehension.

Ultimately, there appears to be a direct causal link between drama-based instruction and reading comprehension (Rose, Parks, Androes, & McMahon, 2001). It appears that because theater students participate in theater programs, they are more likely to increase in their reading engagement and close reading abilities across the content areas (Nageldinger, 2014). Theater students disclosed that when they are involved in a directing activity, they read a script an average of 12 times, and when acting, that number almost doubled to 22. If repeated reading matters in developing fluency, then involvement in theater is a powerful way to promote it.

But beyond the purpose of developing fluency, these readers reported that they were reading multiple times for other important purposes as well: to represent with deep meanings. The actors reread closely and critically to uncover clues about their character and to find out what or whose "voice" drove the decisions their characters made. In the process of becoming fluent, they were exercising an authentic form of close reading, one of the Common Core's anchor standards.

Fluency as a performing art is nowhere as obvious as it is in a typical backstage environment. In any given theater, actors mill around with scripts in hand practicing different ways of saying the same line. During early read throughs, they follow along, waiting for their turn to read their lines. Notes are often provided that focus on enhancing the meaning of the performance and, depending on the director and length of the script, the script may be read though again that day. Then, the actors take the script home, where they will study it with an eye for the broad brush strokes of the plot and then the finer nuances of their characters. As they read through the script, they may note difficult passages to remind them how to vocalize in a way that best represents how they think the line character should "say" each line.

We are not suggesting that you turn your classroom into a theater, but teachers could regard reading and reading fluency instruction as a "performance art." Seeing fluency as an art, and especially a performance art, can open the door for building fluency.

CLOSING COMMENTS

An ideal classroom setting, in our opinion, is one where the instructional activities done in the classroom reflect real-life activities done outside the school. Fluency instruction that is based on making students read fast has little relevance or connection to real life. However, when we think of repeated readings and assisted reading as forms of rehearsal, we can readily see a connection to life outside the classroom. Actor, singers, and poets rehearse or engage in repeated and assisted readings. Their purpose in rehearsal is not to read fast but to communicate meaning and satisfaction to an audience. This artful approach to rehearsal and fluency instruction has many positive outcomes. Students improve in all aspects of fluency—word recognition automaticity and prosody—and because fluency is a foundational competency for comprehension, comprehension also improves. Taking an artful approach to fluency is one that teachers and students find engaging, enjoyable, and worthwhile. We hope that as you make fluency instruction an integral part of your reading curriculum, you come to think of yourself not so much as a scientist doing something artistic but as a reading artist whose performance is backed up by science.

CHAPTER 6

Fluency and the Struggling Reader: Integrated Fluency Instruction

Usually, when we discuss students who have reading difficulties, we get firsthand reports from the students' teachers. They tell us what sort of interventions they are employing with the students and how the students are responding to these instructions. During one of these teacher–student sessions, we received a report from a parent whose 4th-grade child was enrolled in our reading clinic; this child had struggled with reading since kindergarten. "What are the teachers doing with their students?" Mrs. Martinez, the concerned parent, asked.

At first, we thought something was amiss with the instruction. Then, when Mrs. Martinez saw the puzzled looks on our faces, she explained further:

> For 4 years, Kevin has hated reading and reading instruction.
> At first, he struggled with learning to sound out words during
> phonics instruction. Later, he had trouble with the words
> in stories. He read slower than his classmates and he didn't
> understand what he was reading. I have to admit it was painful
> to listen to him read, and he knew it. Poor guy, he got extra
> help in reading in school, but it was mainly more of the same.
> More phonics instruction, except it was slower and it wasn't real
> reading. Lots of worksheets that did not involve reading.
> Now in your reading camp, he and I are seeing progress like
> we have never seen before. First of all, he likes it! Every day
> he learns a new poem or song. He can read it well. In fact, he
> reads it to me. Well, he is supposed to read it to me (and his
> dad) several times each evening. And he likes doing it. For the
> first time in his life, he is able to read a poem or other passage
> really well. He reads with very few errors and he uses his voice

to make it sound good. In fact, when he reads his daily poem to us at night, he often changes his voice or pace or pausing to change how the whole poem sounds. Six weeks ago, Kevin was a kid who did not believe in himself as reader. Today, although he still struggles, he at least sees that he is able to read short passages as well as anyone in his class. His confidence in himself has just soared. And that has led to more reading on his own. Just the other day, he asked me to take him to the library so that he could find some stories to read on his own. So that is why I asked the question just what are the teachers doing? I meant it as a compliment.

Actually, Mrs. Martinez knew what was going on in her son's reading group; she was just so amazed at how Kevin had responded that she wondered out loud if there was something else going on. There was indeed some intense fluency instruction going on.

In this chapter, we explore how we can help students who find reading difficult and for whom some aspect of fluency is a major contributing source of the problem. Because fluency—or, we should say, the lack of appropriate levels of fluency—is a common characteristic of students who struggle from the earliest stages of reading into the secondary grades (Paige, Rasinski, & Maguri-Lavell, 2012; Valencia & Buly, 2004), it is vital to understand the full consequences of difficulties in reading fluency.

Students who struggle with reading often never experience the sense of accomplishment that comes from reading a text well. Typically, a teacher will assign these students a text. When the students who struggle with reading try to read it, they often will have many word recognition errors, excessively slow reading rates, or poor expression. Once the students "complete" that reading, followed by a discussion and extension activity, they move on to a new passage and relive the negative reading experience again. Eventually, after this happens enough times in the classroom, these students will no longer see themselves as good readers, and subsequently, they will begin to lose confidence, become discouraged, and avoid reading.

Like these "hypothetical" students, we've all struggled with something we are not very good at doing. And, like these students, after we have proven to ourselves that we perform poorly at that activity, we usually avoid doing it. We have little desire to repeat the negative experience. Yet, when students begin to avoid reading, the consequences tend to be more severe. If they don't improve their reading skills, their reading development will lag behind that of their peers and they may never develop the lifelong reading habits that we want for all students.

THINK ABOUT IT

Think of some task that you have convinced yourself you simply have little or no aptitude for. (For Tim, it is generally anything mechanical or that involves tools.) Have you attempted the task in the past? What happened in these attempts? Do you still engage in the task with the same level of frequency as you have in the past? Our guess is that you at least tacitly avoid that task. (In Tim's case, he actively avoids most mechanical work, because, when he has tried to fix things that involved tools, he actually created even more problems that had to be solved by a real expert—his wife!) If you are reading this book with others, share your experiences. Do you think your experiences are analogous to what might happen for students who don't experience much success in reading? Now think of something at which you are good and in which you find satisfaction. Do you avoid opportunities to engage in those activities?

WHAT WE THINK

We are fairly well convinced that negative experiences set up a negative reinforcement cycle. In this cycle, students find less and less satisfaction with an activity and eventually refrain from engaging in it because of their lack of success. This lack of success in reading then translates into a lack of success in school, which can lead to poor performance in other curricular areas or even to school dropout.

When we engage in activities in which we display talent, we often engage in them more and more often, sometimes escalating the challenge level of the task. Because we find satisfaction in doing the task, we long to continue working at the task because we will continue to improve.

HELPING STUDENTS ACHIEVE SUCCESS IN READING

So, a major goal for working with struggling readers is to have them experience the success in reading that their more advanced reading classmates have experienced from the beginning of their school days. This is why fluency instruction is imperative for their development.

In the immediately preceding chapters, we described methods or approaches to fluency instruction. These included modeling fluent reading, assisted reading (where students read a text while simultaneously hearing a version of the text read to them), and practicing or rehearsing. As you will see in Chapter 7, these activities, which are highly appropriate for school settings, can easily be integrated into home programs as well.

By themselves, these instructional approaches have great potential for improving various aspects of fluency. However, when the elements are combined, they lead to an instructional benefit that is greater than the sum of the parts. The opportunity for a student to listen to a text read fluently, then rehearse reading the text (first while simultaneously listening to a fluent rendering of the text and then on her or his own), and eventually perform for an audience of some sort allows each instructional element to interact with and facilitate the other elements. This yields three results: (1) gains in fluency on the passage practiced; (2) a sense of success over the passage practiced (the modeling and rehearsal eventually gets students to the point at which they can read the text well); and (3) gains in fluency on new passages. If such an approach can be done as a regular classroom or clinical routine, the accelerative gains are not only seen from the beginning to the end of the lesson but also from one lesson to the next.

We call this an integrated or synergistic approach to fluency instruction. One such approach we have developed is the Fluency Development Lesson (FDL). The FDL is essentially a quick lesson in which students learn to read one text well per lesson. In order to help students achieve mastery of a text in a short time, the teacher employs those elements of fluency instruction previously mentioned. He or she reads the text to students, reads the text with students, and finally allows students to rehearse or engage in repeated readings of the passage. Through this process, students reach a point at which they are able to read the text well. Students then perform the text for an audience, engage in a study of words from the text, and continue practicing the text or a related version of it at home with parents and family members.

In essence, the FDL is a version of the traditional primary grade activity in which students develop fluent reading by learning and performing a poem or other short text over the course of several days. On the final day, when they are able to read it well, the students perform it for another classroom, parents, or others. The major difference between this common classroom activity and the FDL is that the FDL compresses the entire week into one lesson and is much more intentional in terms of its nature and goals. Students who struggle in reading are generally well behind their average and above-average reading classmates. Struggling readers require scaffolded instruction that is more intense than what their more average-achieving classmates receive; otherwise, they may never catch up. The FDL is intended to be implemented several times per week (daily would be ideal). Thus, in the course of one 5-day instructional week, students receiving FDL instruction would essentially receive the equivalent of 5 weeks of the more common classroom fluency activity. Intensity is also achieved through the intentional and synergistic integration in one lesson of known fluency approaches—modeling fluent reading of text, assisted reading of a text, and repeated reading of the text.

The actual protocol for implementing the FDL is provided below:

- **Materials Needed:** Daily short text (poem, song lyric, segment from a story, and so forth—50–250 words in length). Make two copies for each student and a display copy on chart paper or another display device.
- **Time Needed:** Approximately 15–30 minutes per day, depending on the length and challenge of the text. It could occur at the beginning of the day, before lunch, or during the regular reading period; this approach can also be employed in clinical settings.
- **Lesson Sequence:**
  1. The teacher introduces a new text and reads it to the students two or three times while the students listen or follow along silently. The text can be a poem, segment from the reading program or trade book selection, and so on. The teacher can change the prosodic nature of his or her reading from one reading to the next.
  2. Teacher and students discuss the nature and content of the passage as well as the quality of teacher's readings of the passage. Which one of the readings did students find most fluent? Why?
  3. Teacher and students read the passage chorally several times. Antiphonal reading and other choral variations (such as alternate lines) are used to create variety and maintain engagement.

4. The teacher organizes students into pairs or trios. Each student practices the passage two to four times while his or her partner listens and provides support and encouragement. The goal is to reach a point at which the students are able to read the text fluently and meaningfully.

5. Individuals and groups of students perform their reading for the class or other audience such as another class, a parent visitor, the school principal, or another teacher. Students can also record their reading for later playback or to be archived.

6. After having practiced the text several times, students may have the text or a portion of the text memorized and thus may not be sufficiently focusing on the words. So, following (or prior to) the performance (step 5 above), the students and their teacher engage in a study of some of the words from the text. The teacher and students choose (harvest) four to eight words they think are interesting from the text to add to the individual students' word banks and/or the classroom word wall. The words on the classroom word wall are read daily by students. The teacher encourages students to use the words in their own oral and written language.

7. The teacher leads the students in 5–10 minutes of word study activities. The word study activities can take a variety of forms. Here are a few:

   a. Play a word game using the chosen (and other) words (for example, Wordo—word bingo).

   b. Sort the words by various features (syllable, presence of consonant blend).

   c. Expand on certain word families present in the chosen words. For example, if the word *gold* was harvested, the teacher can point out the *–old* word family and brainstorm other words that contain that pattern (such as *bold, fold, oldest, cold, mold, hold, sold*).

   d. Engage in a word building exercise in which new words are created by changing, adding, subtracting, or rearranging letters from a given word. Here's an example:

   Gold Change one letter to make another word for "brave."

   Bold Change one letter to make a word referring to a person who has lost the hair on the top of the head.

   Bald Change one letter to make a word meaning a round object used for play.

Ball Change one letter to make a word that means an indoor shopping center.

Mall Change one letter to make a word referring to a place where grain is turned into flour.

Mill Change one letter to make a word for a drink that comes from cows.

Milk

8. The students take a copy of the passage home to practice with parents and other family members. The other copy is left in their fluency notebook for further practice.

9. The following day students read the passage from the previous day as a group or to their teacher or to a fellow student to check for accuracy and fluency. Words from the previous day are also read, reread, grouped, and sorted by students and groups of students.

10. The instructional routine then begins again with step 1 using a new passage.

If this routine were done daily, students would definitely improve in their word recognition accuracy, vocabulary, and fluency. And because these are the foundations for comprehension, then the students' reading comprehension would improve as well. Moreover, because students are mastering a text daily, they are more likely to view themselves as persons who are able to master reading. As a result, their confidence in themselves and the satisfaction they take in their reading abilities increases remarkably.

The protocol presented above should be thought of as a general outline. There is plenty of room for adaptation and variation. First, variation can occur in the type of text chosen. You should choose materials that you think your students can master in a short period of intense practice. However, the text can actually take a variety of forms (see next section for more on text choice). The number of times you read the text to your students, or with your students, or have your students read on their own (as well as the actual nature of the reading) can definitely change from one lesson to the next. Generally, the challenge of the text will guide you as to the number of readings the students should do. More-challenging material requires more practice. Some teachers extend the lesson over 2 days if they feel more practice is necessary or if they are in a daily time crunch. In some instances, in order to increase the acceleration, the lesson can be implemented twice a day (with different texts for each lesson). The performance activity can be delayed until the end of the week where students choose the text they wish to perform for the weekly classroom poetry slam or reading festival. The point we wish to make is that you, the teacher, are free to adapt the lesson to make it fit your needs and the needs of your students. What we would like for you to keep in mind in your adaptations are those essential elements of modeling fluent reading, assisted reading, and repeated reading, as well as maintaining a level of intensity (daily or near-daily use of the FDL) of the routine in order to accelerate each student's progress in reading.

THE MATTER OF TEXTS

We have found that the choice of texts we ask students to read in the FDL is critical to its success. In many if not most fluency programs, students are asked to read informational texts repeatedly. Though we recognize the importance of informational texts, we feel they may not be the best choice for fluency practice and development. Informational texts do not easily lend themselves to oral expressive reading, thus limiting their effectiveness in developing expression, or prosody.

We think the teacher should choose texts that are performance based or for read-aloud to an audience for fluency activities. If a text is meant to be performed, it has to be rehearsed. Rehearsal is a form of repeated reading. When students rehearse performance texts, they do not focus on the speed of reading but on expressive reading. Texts such as expressive story segments, scripts for Readers Theatre, song lyrics, poetry, speeches, dialogues, and monologues are more appropriate for fluency development.

For the FDL, however, we think poetry in particular is the text of choice for several reasons. First, poetry for children is relatively short. You need short texts for the FDL because students will be reading the text multiple times over a short period. Poetry has rhythm and rhyme embedded in it that aid in learning to read the text and increase the enjoyment of reading. Because poems often rhyme, the rhyming words can used for word family instruction (for example, *pot–hot* in "Pease Porridge Hot"). Poems contain rich vocabulary as well as meaning that often require thoughtful and close analysis. And, as we mentioned earlier, because poems are meant to be performed, students have a natural or authentic reason to engage in repeated readings of a poem.

One more thing about poetry: With the rise of the Internet, poetry for children is easily accessible for teachers. (In Appendixes B through E, we provide a list of some of our favorite websites for finding poetry and other fluency texts.)

In our reading clinic, over the course of 5 weeks, students developed a repertoire of 25–50 poems and other short texts that they can read and understand fluently. On the final day of the clinic, the students read and perform poetry and other texts they had been learning during our clinic session. The pride they have in such an accomplishment is obvious as they share their performance texts.

THINK ABOUT IT

Based on what we have presented, what do you think of the FDL as an intervention for your struggling readers? We will share some evidence later, but we think you may want to experience a version of the FDL yourself. Here's how. You will need a partner to work with on this. In your most "fluent" voice, please read the "Jerseywocky" text, which is a New Jersey parody of the poem "Jabberwocky" by Lewis Carroll. Have your partner count the number of words you read correctly in the first minute of your reading. Write this number down; it is your pretest score.

"Jerseywocky" by Paul Kieffer

'Twas Bergen and the Erie road
Did Mahwah into Paterson;
All Jersey were the Ocean Groves
And the Red Bank Bayonne.

"Beware the Hopatcong, my son!
The teeth that bite! The nails that claw!
Beware the Bound Brook bird, and shun
The Kearney Communipaw!"

He took his Belmar blade in hand,
Long time the Folsom foe he sought,
Till rested he by a Bayway tree
And stood awhile in thought.

And as in Nutley thought he stood,
The Hopatcong, with eyes of flame,
Came Whippany through the Englewood
And Garfield as it came.

One two! one two! and through and through
The Belmar blade went Hackensack!
He left it dead, and with its head
He went Weehawken back.

"And hast though slain the Hopatcong?
Come to my arms, my Perth Amboy!
Hohokus day! Soho! Rahway!"
He Caldwell in his joy.

'Twas Bergen and the Erie road
Did Mahwah into Paterson;
All Jersey were the Ocean Groves
And the Red Bank Bayonne.

Now, we'd like for you to do a quick FDL on the original "Jabberwocky" poem. Have your partner read "Jabberwocky" to you while you follow along silently; talk about the meaning of the poem. Next, read the poem with your partner chorally, and then read the poem to your partner while your partner follows along silently and tells you what he or she liked about your reading. Then do a bit of word study. Choose 10 interesting words from "Jabberwocky" with your partner and discuss what instructional activities you might do with the words that would be fun.

"Jabberwocky" by Lewis Carroll (1897)

'Twas brillig, and the slithy toves
 Did gyre and gimble in the wabe:
All mimsy were the borogoves,
 And the mome raths outgrabe.

"Beware the Jabberwock, my son!
 The jaws that bite, the claws that catch!

Beware the Jubjub bird, and shun
 The frumious Bandersnatch!"

He took his vorpal sword in hand:
Long time the manxome foe he sought --
So rested he by the Tumtum tree,
And stood awhile in thought.

And, as in uffish thought he stood,
The Jabberwock, with eyes of flame,
Came whiffling through the tulgey wood,
And burbled as it came!

One, two! One, two! And through and through
The vorpal blade went snicker-snack!
He left it dead, and with its head
He went galumphing back.

"And, has thou slain the Jabberwock?
Come to my arms, my beamish boy!
O frabjous day! Callooh! Callay!"
He chortled in his joy.

`Twas brillig, and the slithy toves
Did gyre and gimble in the wabe;
All mimsy were the borogoves,
And the mome raths outgrabe.

Did you notice your reading of "Jabberwocky" improve as you practiced it? Of course, that is to be expected. If you practice a text, you
tend to get better at reading it. Let's see, though, if your practice on
"Jabberwocky" led to an improvement of your reading of "Jerseywocky."
Go back to "Jerseywocky" and read it again using the same protocol as
you did in the pretest. Have your partner determine the number of words
you read in 1 minute. Now, because you have already read "Jerseywocky"
once, your second reading of it should improve. But how much improvement will you experience? When we have done this exercise (pretest and
posttest of "Jerseywocky") without the practice of "Jabberwocky," we
found that readers improved by 5 to 10 words in their second reading.

So, did you improve your second reading of "Jerseywocky" by more than 10 words? Were you able to read "Jerseywocky" with fewer errors? Were you able to read "Jerseywocky" with better expression or prosody? Think about it. What does this mean?

WHAT WE THINK

Our experience has been that after adults engage in this abbreviated form of the FDL on "Jabberwocky" they are able to read 20 or more words on their second reading of "Jerseywocky." It is not uncommon for our adults to read 40 more words on their second reading of "Jerseywocky." What we think is happening is that your practice of "Jabberwocky" is helping you develop accuracy, automaticity, and prosody on "Jabberwocky." But there was some carryover to "Jerseywocky," too. Not only did the FDL on "Jabberwocky" improve your fluency on "Jerseywocky," but it likely improved your comprehension of "Jerseywocky" as you were able to devote more of your attention to making meaning, rather than decoding words.

We admit that the two poems are highly correlated in their structure and this correlation is part of the reason for the carryover improvement. But you might also recall that you only practiced "Jabberwocky" three times. In a true FDL, you would have practiced your text anywhere from 6 to 15 times. Imagine the improvements students would make if they had such intense practice for short periods of time on a regular (daily) basis. The gains made on one day would carry over to the next day and the next. Over the course of several months of doing the FDL daily, we think you could bring your students up several grade levels in their fluency. And this, of course, would also lead to significant improvements in reading comprehension.

THE FDL IN ACTION

Daily and consistent employment of the Fluency Development Lesson can lead to significant improvements in various aspects of reading. The Kent State University (KSU) reading clinic works with elementary and middle school students who are experiencing difficulty in reading for a 5-week period during the summer session. When the clinic begins, students are initially tested to determine the primary source of their difficulties. We have found that reading fluency tends to be the major cause of difficulty for a significant majority of students. Thus, the Fluency Development Lesson has become a core instructional method used in the clinic.

Two recent studies (Zimmerman, Rasinski, Kruse, Was, Dunlosky, & Rawson, 2012; Zimmerman, Rasinski, & Melewski, 2013) of students who attended the KSU clinic have demonstrated that the students receiving the FDL treatment made significant and substantial gains over the course of the clinical program in word recognition and fluency. Moreover, because proficiency in word recognition and fluency are necessary conditions for comprehension, gains in comprehension were also found. Teachers employing the FDL report being enthusiastic about its use as they see students who previously were making minimal gains in reading achievement significantly accelerate their reading progress. Although our own work with the FDL has been in clinical settings, we have found it to be easily and effectively adapted for classroom instruction as well (Rasinski, Padak, Linek, & Sturtevant, 1994).

CLOSING COMMENTS

We continue to have significant numbers of students in the United States and elsewhere who struggle in reading. Recent research has shown that reading fluency is an area of major concern for a large number of these students. If fluency is a source of concern, then intensive instruction to overcome fluency problems is called for. The Fluency Development Lesson is a simple and efficient approach to fluency instruction that has been shown to improve fluency and overall reading proficiency. We are becoming increasingly convinced that regular and consistent use of the FDL, as well as other fluency interventions that are based on elements of effective fluency instruction, can make a big impact on the literacy lives of many students who struggle and reduce the number of students who find reading difficult.

CHAPTER 7

Reading Fluency Begins at Home

I (Tim) was an early reader. By the time I started school, I was already able to read much of the material that was part of our 1st-grade reading curriculum. Clearly, my early literacy development was not due to school. Something in my home was happening.

Dolores Durkin's (1966) seminal research found that children who were early readers most likely had parents who read to them regularly. Interestingly, I don't recall my parents reading to me very often. Indeed, I don't recall having many books in my home—books for adults or children. With the help of my mother, I discovered years later how I (and my brother and sister) became readers at home. Although my father was a factory worker, he was also a musician who, with his six-piece band, played gigs at local night clubs and weddings on weekends. It was not unusual for my dad to come home from work, take a quick shower, get his saxophone or clarinet, call his children in from outside, and have a 30-minute jam session several times a week. Actually, it wasn't a jam session at all; it was his rehearsing for his weekend gig, and it was the generally many of the same songs each week. So while he played, my mother would pass out song sheets and we were invited (required) to sing along with him as he played. This was a way for my father to spend time with his children. But, looking at it retrospectively, it became clear that we were engaging in reading (singing) the lyrics to the songs he was playing. Music has always been a large part of my family history and whether it was singing along with my father, singing along with songs on the record player (while following along with the lyrics on the record cover), or singing at family gatherings, those musical experiences were an entry point for reading for myself and my siblings.

My mother also played an important role in my early reading development. In the evenings, after I had said my prayers, she would

sometimes share a poem with me (she had several collections of poetry for adults and children). This sharing took place over several
days. Early in the week, she would read me the poem while I listened. As the week progressed, we went from her reading, to us
reading together, to eventually my being able to read the poem on
my own.

Now, I may only have had the poem memorized, but in many
ways memorization is at the heart of reading. One goal of reading
instruction is to develop students' sight word vocabularies: words that
are instantly and holistically recognized. Sight words are essentially
memorized words—by sight and sound. Many years later, when my
mother had developed Alzheimer's and had difficulty recognizing me
as her son, she could still remember and recite many of the songs and
poems she had read and learned many years earlier.

In both of these cases, through my father's singing and my mother's poetry, I was engaging in many of the components of effective
fluency instruction that were described earlier in this book. First, my
parents modeled the reading of the text by reading or playing the
text while I listened. Later, we engaged in assisted reading as I read
the song lyrics or poems with my mother or other family members.
Finally, I engaged in repeated readings as we sang or read the same
songs and poems over several days (and even weeks). Also, the nature
of the texts that we sang and read lent themselves to my early fluent reading development. The songs and poems were relatively short,
which made them fairly easy to learn. Additionally, these texts were
able to be read with prosody, or expression. The rhythm, rhyme, and
repetition integrated into songs and poems require them to be expressed with appropriate prosody.

Although Tim's case may be a bit out of the ordinary, we have met
many adults who had similar experiences when growing up, which
helped develop their early literacy competencies. As was the case for
Tim, for these adults, these experiences were some of their most cher-
ished childhood memories. In the days before television and computers took on such a dominant place in the lives of families, many
families spent time together reading stories, poetry, prayers, and even
singing songs. These activities have been replaced by time spent in
front of the television or computer screen. There is no reason to think
we cannot encourage and even expect parents to make use of similar
activities in their own families to enrich family life and at the same
time to encourage fluent reading development.

THINK ABOUT IT

Can you recall how your parents and family supported your literacy development? Make a list of those things you recall them doing. Perhaps it was reading to you regularly. What did they read—children's books, the comic section of the newspaper? Did you ever read with your parents? What do you recall reading? Were there lots of books, including children's books, in your home? Did you go to the local library regularly with your family? Were there any writing activities that you remember in your family? Describe them. To what extent can these activities be encouraged in the families whose children you teach? How might you go about initiating and supporting such activities in your students' families?

WHAT WE THINK

In the same way that we often emulate our own parents and others whom we admire, we think it is entirely possible and productive to ask the parents of our students to try to emulate some of those home activities that we know through our own experience promoted our literacy development. The key is to be sensitive and to be willing to allow parents to adapt approaches, so they can fit into the individual circumstances of their own families.

FAMILIES ARE IMPORTANT IN LEARNING TO READ

Although there is general consensus that parents and families are important in children's literacy development, there was a time, about 50 or more years ago, when families were actually discouraged from teaching or nurturing reading in their children. The conventional wisdom at the time was that reading was such a technical and complex understanding that involving parents and families may have negative consequences. We have to wonder if this marginalization of the role of parents years ago is part of the reason why many teachers find it difficult to get parents involved today.

Despite the challenges we have in involving parents, an existing and growing body of research has demonstrated time and time again that parents make a difference in their children's general academic achievement and literacy learning. An international study of reading achievement from several years back (Postlethwaite & Ross,

1992) found, for example, that home and parent involvement was the number-one predictor of 2nd- and 8th-grade reading achievement. Moreover, the second most significant predictor of reading success was the amount of reading done at home (in this study, home-based reading was even more significant than the amount of reading done at school).

Reviews of research of early childhood learning suggest that those experiences lay the foundation for success in acquiring later literacy skills (Scarborough, 2001; Whitehurst & Lonigan, 2001). Moreover, longitudinal studies of home literacy experiences during the kindergarten school year (4- and 5-year-old children) have shown that those experiences predicted reading achievement in grades 1 through 4. The reading competencies associated with home literacy experiences were word recognition, spelling, vocabulary, reading fluency, comprehension, and frequency of reading for pleasure (Sénéchal, 2006; Sénéchal & LeFevre, 2002). Parents engaged in activities that included storybook reading to the children and some direct teaching of words.

Similarly, a key finding of Durkin's (1966) own seminal study of children who learned to read before beginning school was that the parents of these early readers read to their children. Interestingly, the small advantage these students had over their non–early reading classmates actually increased as students moved on to higher grade levels.

It seems clear, then, that parents and families make a difference, and the earlier we can involve parents and families in children's literacy development, the more likely the children will benefit. Additionally, it seems more likely that parents will feel comfortable and competent to be involved in their children's reading development during the early school years. In the following sections, we describe ways in which parents and families, with the guidance and support of teachers, can help students become more-fluent readers to improve their overall reading achievement.

PARENTS CAN READ *TO* THEIR CHILDREN

As mentioned earlier, parents reading to their children can be a powerful tool for improving various aspects of students' reading. Parents reading to children can have a particularly powerful effect on children's understanding of and development in reading fluency.

Yet, before we can achieve specific goals for students, we need to understand what the goals are, especially when considering fluency.

For students to become fluent readers, they first need a good sense of what fluency looks and sounds like. When parents read to their children in a fluent, expressive, and confident manner, they are providing for their children a model of fluent reading. Moreover, when parents talk with their children about the nature of their fluent reading, students are more likely to develop a sense of how they themselves should read. The steps for guiding parents in reading fluently to their children are outlined below.

HOW PARENTS CAN READ FLUENTLY TO THEIR CHILDREN

1. Choose books or other reading materials that lend themselves to expressive oral reading. Look for books that contain plenty of dialogue between characters. Look for texts such as poetry that are meant to be read aloud and with good expression.
2. Before reading to your child, look the text over and identify sections that can be read in different voices or with different levels of expression.
3. Practice reading the text on your own. Make sure you are able to read the text at an appropriate rate and with a level of expression that adds to the interest of the text.
4. Read the text to your child or children. Enjoy the experience. Notice how your child gets absorbed into the story as you read it with good fluency.
5. After reading the text to your child, talk about the story and your reading of it with your child. Talking about the story will help your child develop comprehension. Talking about your reading will assist the child's development of fluency. Have your child notice those areas where you used your voice to add to the reading. Help your child notice where you had a dramatic pause, increased or slowed down your reading rate, or read in the voice of a particular character. Ask your child how your reading with expression influenced his or her listening experience.
6. Occasionally, reread short portions of the text in a nonfluent manner (for example, in a monotone, too fast or too slow, with minimal attention to punctuation, and so forth). Talk with your child about how the lack of fluency influenced his or her understanding of and satisfaction with the story itself.
7. Focus on your own expression as you read aloud to your child regularly.

PARENTS CAN READ *WITH* THEIR CHILDREN

In an earlier chapter, we discussed the notion of assisted reading, whereby a student reads a text while simultaneously hearing a fluent reading of the same text. Through the assistance provided by the fluent reading of text, students will approximate the fluent reading not only on the text they are currently reading but on other passages as well. Although such experiences can be offered in school, they can easily be adapted for the home.

Keith Topping (1987a, 1987b, 1989), an English school psychologist, developed a program called "Paired Reading," which was originally developed as an assisted reading program for parents and their children. Implementation of Paired Reading is quite simple; parents can be trained in implementing it in about an hour. The essential elements of implementing Paired Reading are outlined below.

HOW PARENTS CAN DO PAIRED READING

1. You and your child should reserve 10–20 minutes for a minimum of 4 days per week for at least 6 weeks.
2. Your child chooses the text he or she wishes to read. The text can be for pleasure reading or school-assigned reading.
3. You and your child sit comfortably side by side and read the text together simultaneously at a comfortable and conversational reading rate. Adjust your voice and rate to match the child's.
4. As you read with your child, either you or your child should point to the text in order to visually orient to the written text.
5. Set up a simple nonverbal signal with your child. A tap on the wrist or a gentle elbow in the ribs works well. Your child can signal when he or she wishes to read without you. He or she can also use the signal to indicate when he or she wants you to join back in the reading. While your child reads solo, you can read silently or in a low "mumble" voice that slightly trails your child's reading.
6. If, while your child is soloing, he or she runs into some difficulty, such as having trouble decoding a word, you should simply rejoin the reading, stating the correct pronunciation of the difficult word and then continuing to read with your child. Do not stop the reading for a quick lesson in word decoding, as this will disrupt the flow of the reading. You can make a mental note of the difficulty and return to it with a brief discussion at the end of the reading.

7. You may wish to set up a second nonverbal signal for when your child wants you to read, with him or her following along silently. Try to minimize this sort of reading, as you want your child to do the bulk of the reading.

8. Read together to a predetermined spot in the text (about 10–15 minutes). Be sure to discuss the reading with your child—both the content of the text and also how your child felt about his or her reading.

Paired Reading is a deceptively simple activity that employs real reading in a very natural setting. Yet because of the support parents are providing their child and because of the increased volume of reading the child is doing, the child is likely to make extraordinary growth in fluency as well as other aspects of reading. One study found that the use of Paired Reading over the course of 2-and-a-half months resulted in students making gains of at least 6 months in reading (Limbrick, McNaughton, & Cameron, 1985). A 6-week (20 minutes per night) implementation of Paired Reading with students identified as struggling readers resulted in gains of 7 months to a year in both word recognition accuracy and reading comprehension (Bushnell, Miller, & Robson, 1982). Moreover, the gains students made were still detected 6 months after the program ended. Topping's own review of research related to Paired Reading suggests that students from the primary through secondary grades can make a minimum of three times the expected progress in reading in word recognition and comprehension with the regular use of Paired Reading. That is, children who previously made a half month's progress in reading for every month of instruction prior to using Paired Reading will begin to have gains of 1.5 months' progress for each month of instruction with the inclusion of Paired Reading.

PARENTS CAN LISTEN TO THEIR CHILDREN READ

As much as we might hope that parents read to and with their children, the fact of the matter is that some parents may not be able to read to their children in a fluent manner. And other parents may be reluctant to read to their children because of their own past school experiences. All parents, however, can listen to their children read.

Now, you may not think that parents simply listening to children read could have an impact on their reading. You might even believe that when parents are simply listening, they aren't doing anything that teaches or supports their child's reading. Yet, there is research that finds value in parents listening to their children reading. One study (Wilks & Clarke, 1988) compared the reading outcomes of children whose mothers were given training in how to listen to their children's reading (with a focus on meaning and praise over word prompts) and children with mothers who were not given such training. The children whose mothers were provided support in positive listening made significantly greater gains in both word recognition accuracy and comprehension over the children whose mothers were not provided with such support.

In the study just mentioned, the mothers were given support and training with feedback on focusing more on text meaning when their children read and less on correcting word recognition errors using phonics, choosing appropriate books for children's reading, and encouraging good reading habits. We feel that an additional focus could be on fluent reading. As children read to their parents, some time might be spent talking with the children, before and after the reading, about reading with appropriate expression that reflects the meaning of the text. As the child reads, the parent can monitor the child's oral fluency and provide feedback after the reading. Children learn based on where we focus their attention. If we focus on fluency that reflects meaning, children will develop such a focus in their own independent reading.

HOW TO BE A POSITIVE LISTENER TO YOUR CHILD'S READING

1. Help your child select books (and other reading materials that he or she will find interesting and that he or she is able to read independently).
2. Find a comfortable setting where you can follow along as your child reads to you.
3. Preview the reading with your child. Note headings and illustrations in text as well as those sections that may require a change in voice during reading.
4. As your child reads to you, try to avoid asking your child to "sound out" difficult words. Rather, help your child focus on the context of

the text where the difficulty is located. Invite him or her to make a prediction of what the word may be based on the context and the sound–symbol relationships in the word.

5. Stop at appropriate spots in the reading to summarize the meaning of the text. Encourage your child to make predictions about what may happen next in the passage.

6. At the end of the reading, discuss the meaning of the content just read. Spend a bit of time also talking about how your child actually read the text. Did he or she read with good volume that indicated confidence in his or her reading? Did he or she read with good and meaningful expression? Did he or she change his or her voice at appropriate parts of the passage? Did he or she attend to punctuation? Was the reading done at an appropriate pace? Focus on the positive aspects of your child's oral reading.

FAST START IN READING

We have good evidence that reading to children, reading with children, and listening to children read at home (as well as school) can have a significant and positive impact on children's reading development. (If nothing else, these elements add to the total volume of print exposure for students.) If adults combine these elements into an integrated lesson, it has the potential for accelerating children's progress even more. A combined and integrated lesson could have an impact that is greater than the sum of the elements individually. Certainly, when children listen to someone reading a passage to them, then read it with assistance, and eventually read it on their own, they are engaging in a form of repeated reading. Moreover, they will be able to read a new text reasonably well, a text that they had previously not been able to read fluently. Recognizing the potential of an integrated approach for fostering fluency and overall reading development, as well as the importance of home involvement in literacy and knowing of our own home literacy experiences, Nancy Padak and Tim Rasinski (2004) developed a reading fluency program that can be implemented either at home or in school. The program is called Fast Start because it was intended to be a great way to get students off to a quick and successful start in their literacy development.

The Fast Start program is actually a trimmed-down version of the Fluency Development Lesson we described earlier in this book. Essentially, the goal of Fast Start is for children to learn to read a new and short text (usually a poem or nursery rhyme) over the course of a day or two. We have broken the actual lesson down into several steps that mirror those instructional elements previously described and can be stated as a chant for easy memorization: Read to, read with, listen to your child read!

Read to . . .

Imagine a student coming home from kindergarten or a 1st-grade student coming home from school twice a week with a sheet of paper that contains a short children's poem, like "Little Bo Peep" or "Jack and Jill." After having an after-school snack, Mom or Dad sits down next to the child and reads the selected rhyme to the child in a clear voice, where every word can be distinctly heard. The parents also point to the words as they are read. Following a brief conversation about the content and words in the poem as well as how the parent may have read the poem, the parent reads the text to the child one or two more times, often changing some aspect of his or her reading. This may include changes in volume, expression, pacing, or even accent. The intent is to keep the child's interest in and attention to the text high.

Read with . . .

After several readings by the parent, the child is asked to join in the next two or three readings of assigned rhyme. Again, variation in the ways that the text is read by parent and child maintains engagement. Some variations in the reading include the following: Parent reads loudly, child reads softly; child reads loudly, parent softly; alternate lines; use high pitch or low pitch; fast reading or slow reading. Throughout the readings, the parent or child points to the words in the text as they are read in order to keep attention focused on the text itself.

Listen to Your Child Read

After the parent has read the text to the child multiple times and then reads the text with the child several more times, it is very likely that the child will be able to recite the rhyme, or at least a portion of it, on his or her own with some assistance from the parent. The parent may then ask the child to read the text several times for different purposes, or different audiences, or in different voices.

Word Study

Often, after several readings, children may have the text that they have read repeatedly memorized. And so, when reading the text to the parent, the child may not be tracking the words as closely as he or she needs to order to improve word recognition. Thus, a fourth step in Fast Start is a word study component in which the parent and child choose a set of 5 to 10 words they find interesting. Those words are the focus of study for the next 5 or so minutes. Activities may include the parent explaining the words to the child, using the words in sentences to demonstrate contextual meaning, focusing on sounds and letters, and exploring and expanding on particular word families. For example, for "Little Bo Peep," the two rhyming words *peep* and *sheep* could be among the 5 to 10 words chosen. Then, the parent could point out the *–eep* word family in both of these words and brainstorm other words in the *–eep* word family—*jeep, beep, seep, creep, steep, weep, keep, sleep, sweep, deep, steeple, keeper*, and so on. All the words could be listed on a sheet of paper and practiced over the next several days.

The chosen and brainstormed words could also be used for family game-like activities, such as Concentration or WORDO. In Concentration, or match games, one word is written on a small card. On separate cards, the same words are written a second time. All cards are laid facedown randomly on a grid. Players take turns trying to match the words up by uncovering two at a time. In WORDO, students are given a sheet on which a blank 5 x 5 matrix is printed (see Figure 7.1). Children randomly write one word in each box. If there are not enough word family words to fill each box, the parent or teacher may ask for additional other words to be used. Once all the cards are filled in, the parent or teacher will call out a word or definition and the child will have to find the appropriate word on the grid. The word is marked. When a player has five words marked in a row—across or diagonally—WORDO is called and a small prize is awarded.

Figure 7.1. WORDO Card

W	O	R	D	O

Certainly, you can see that by the end of the lesson the child can read the poem reasonably well. More important, when these activities are done on a consistent and regular basis (four to five times per week), the child's reading and reading fluency growth can easily be accelerated. Moreover, the consistency, simplicity, and brevity of the program make it easy for parents to learn and implement with their children. Finally, Fast Start has adaptability. In the previous paragraphs, we have outlined the components of the program. We do not intend for these components and their implementation to be taken prescriptively. There are many ways teachers and parents can adapt the program for their own use to work around their own personal circumstances. For example, the lesson itself could be drawn out over 2 days instead of 1. If parents cannot do four to five lessons per week, then perhaps they can do one or two. Instead of poems, parents may choose texts that are more culturally appropriate, such as religious prayers or stories. Of course, the children's growth may be affected by such adaptations, but growth will still be apparent.

DOES FAST START WORK?

We developed Fast Start as a simple and quick way for parents to help their children develop the foundational skills of fluency and word recognition that are essential for deeper and more-sophisticated levels of literacy. Of course, a literacy program is only valuable to the extent to which it actually delivers on its promise. Over the years, several reports have demonstrated the value of Fast Start (Padak & Rasinski, 2004; Rasinski, 1995; Rasinski & Stevenson, 2005). These studies have found that Fast Start was associated with improvements in word recognition and fluency with young students. Moreover, parents and children who used the program were overwhelmingly positive in their evaluation. Parents appreciated the quick and predictable routine, and both parents and children enjoyed the opportunity to spend a few minutes together regularly to share and learn to read a poem or other text.

Sue Ann Crosby is a reading intervention teacher for kindergarten and 1st grade at K. R. Hanchey Elementary School in Beauregard Parish School Board, Louisiana. She has worked with 1st-grade teachers since 2008 in training and guiding parents in the use of Fast Start with 1st-grade students. The results of her school's use of Fast Start have been remarkable (Crosby, Rasinski, Padak, & Yildirim, 2014). What is particularly notable about her school's use of the program is that it has not been a 1-year-and-done activity. The teachers and principal at Hanchey Elementary have been committed to using Fast Start yearly. As a result, parent participation in Fast Start has increased with each succeeding year. In the first year, no parents engaged in more than 22 Fast Start lessons with their children. In the second year, 7 parents had completed more than 31 lessons, and by the third year, 20 parents of 1st-grade students did a minimum of 31 lessons. The overall average number of Fast Start lessons completed also increased over the first 3 years of the project, from 11 lessons in year 1, to 19 lessons in year 2, and to 31 lessons in year 3.

The increased use of Fast Start also corresponded to substantial improvement in 1st-graders' fluency and word recognition. For example, students whose parents engaged them in 10 lessons or fewer in years 2 and 3 of the project exhibited an average oral reading fluency gain of 68 words correct per minute from the beginning of the year to the end. Students whose parents completed 31 or more Fast Start lessons had an average oral reading fluency gain of 88 words correct per minute, a 29% improvement over the students with less Fast Start involvement. Keep in mind, also, that all students had very similar instruction in school, and the only significant difference between the two groups was their parents' work with them on Fast Start. Moreover, parents felt that the use of Fast Start benefited their children; 90% of all 1st-grade parents in the 3-year implementation of Fast Start agreed that the program was beneficial for their children.

FAST START FOR OLDER STUDENTS

As the name implies, Fast Start is intended for children who are just at the beginning stages of formal or conventional reading. However, because many upper elementary, middle, and high school students also struggle with fluency, the Fast Start concept can easily be adapted for older students. The key element for adapting the program for older students is to find material that is appropriate for their ages and interests. Clearly, there is plenty of poetry and other such texts that would easily appeal to older students. Another adaptation is how the text practice can be done at home. Parents can certainly provide the bulk of the practice; however, with the use of technology, students can practice the daily text while listening to a fluent podcast made by the teacher and posted on the classroom website.

CLOSING COMMENTS

We all come to literacy in different ways. For many children, reading begins informally at home as parents begin to read storybooks to their children. This is a wonderful way to move children into the world of literacy. For other families, such as my own, the introduction to literacy can take less traveled roads. Literacy can begin with poetry, songs, and even reading the environmental print that children see in their everyday lives. Regardless of how literacy happens, the fact is that parents can play an incredibly important role in developing those foundational competencies of word recognition and fluency as well as developing an early love for reading and written words.

In this chapter, we encourage you to take a more intentional approach to parent involvement in literacy. Developing and implementing school-based family programs that involve parents consistently reading to their children, reading with their children, and/or listening to their children read, as well as engaging in word exploration and play, has the potential not only to get students off to a fast start in reading but also to develop a school–home literacy culture that will, no doubt, improve the literacy outcomes for many students who may otherwise fall between the cracks.

CHAPTER 8

Your Turn

So far in this book we have invited you to take another look at reading fluency—why it is important and how it can be taught. We have also provided real-life examples of teachers who have made fluency an important part of their literacy curriculum. In Chapter 2, we provided an overview of reading fluency and described how fluency has evolved in schools' reading curricula over time. In Chapter 3, we described what has been done in the past to measure fluency and where our current understandings have brought us in terms of assessment. A teacher-friendly and efficient approach to assessing fluency was introduced along with progress monitoring tools to keep track of growth.

In Chapter 4, we presented essential methods for teaching reading fluency that have been shown to be effective through published research as well as through actual classroom practice, including our own. In Chapter 5, we focused on how fluency can been seen and practiced as an art as well as a science, and, in Chapter 6, we explored how to help students who need a more intensive, yet still authentic and engaging, approach to fluency development by sharing with you the Fluency Development Lesson, a simple but effective intervention that we have used in our own work with struggling readers to great effect.

Finally, Chapter 7 brought the concepts full circle by showing how teachers and school administrators can involve parents and other family members in easy yet quite effective ways to promote and develop fluency in their children. And now, we hand fluency instruction over to you. This chapter serves as a guide for what you can do in your own classroom or instructional setting, beginning tomorrow, to make fluency an integral part of your curriculum to improve the reading outcomes of your students.

Practical considerations of fluency development in the classroom include goals, time, materials, lesson format, and progress monitoring. For exercises that lead to performance, we also consider audience and location.

GOALS

If you wish to make fluency an important part of your curriculum, you first need to think about the goals you may have for students in terms of fluency. First, consider where you want your students to be in terms of word recognition automaticity and prosody at the end of your instruction. Certainly, the automaticity norms provided in Chapter 3 can give you some sense of how the average student performs by grade level and time of year. Goals for prosody may begin with a pre-assessment of students' oral reading expression. If students are considerably below the threshold for appropriate prosodic reading (total score below 10 on the Multidimensional Fluency Scale), then you may identify a goal of moving students to or even above the threshold. If, on the other hand, students are already at or above the threshold, you may simply set a goal for these students to maintain their level of expressiveness in oral reading even on more-challenging texts.

TIME

Time is always a challenge when it comes to instruction, because there never seems to be enough of it. Every year, it seems new requirements are added to the school curriculum, even though the amount of time in school never changes.

If fluency is to be a priority in your curriculum, you need to find time for it. Fortunately, fluency instruction does not need to disrupt an already busy day. Focused fluency instruction, such as the Fluency Development Lesson, can be done in as little as 20 minutes per day. Moreover, if implemented as a regular instructional routine that becomes well known to students, the FDL can be implemented in even less time.

Fluency can easily be integrated into other areas of the curriculum as well. Songs, poetry, scripts, and other fluency-oriented texts can be found to support nearly any area of the curriculum, from social studies to science, to math, to language arts. When practicing and performing such materials, students will also be engaging in close reading of content-area materials.

Much fluency work by students can be done independently. I (Jim) have often come into classrooms where students, having a basic mastery of the text, are working unassisted to practice or rehearse on their own or with classmates. Many teachers we know have developed fluency centers in their classrooms (or in the school library) where students can go to rehearse.

Fluency centers can also be used for repositories for scripts, poems, song lyrics, and other materials that students can peruse. With the addition of computers, the fluency center can be adapted to include audio recordings of texts as well, so that students can engage in assisted reading. The computers can also be used to record students' reading. Student recordings of their reading can be added to their personal literacy portfolio to show growth over time. Additionally, students can add to your collection of recorded texts by rehearsing and recording their own readings of texts that other students could use for assisted reading.

Reading practice is an essential element in developing reading fluency. We often think practice only occurs in school. However, as we pointed out in the last chapter, it can and should also occur at home. When parents act as supportive and encouraging listeners, students

THINK ABOUT IT

Take a minute and picture the times you have had opportunities to use any of the many fluency building activities outlined in this book. Maybe you have had your students read a Readers Theatre script with only one rehearsal or told everyone they had to memorize a poem. Are your students among the fortunate who participate in regular singing activities? Perhaps great speeches have presented themselves in your social studies book only to be read silently. How could you change that in your classroom?

WHAT WE THINK

We think by now you have been able to come up with a dozen ideas about how you can incorporate fluency instruction into your daily routine. You have seen that it is relatively simple, requires minimal preparation, and has proven results; you can see the opportunities in some of the things you already do for fluency development through repeated readings. Perhaps you are already scheming to get some fellow teachers on board. We hope so. Our summer reading clinic at Kent State University is never stronger than when the teachers are swapping ideas and buzzing about the successes they are seeing.

could easily engage in 10–20 minutes of oral reading practice at home each evening.

Fluency can also be integrated into extracurricular activities. Putting on a classroom or school play is a natural way to engage students in meaningful reading practice. Indeed, we have heard that many professional actors struggled in reading. I (Jim) spent 7 years directing theater and time and again came across actors who told me they thought they became better readers once they got involved in theater. For whatever reason—a desire to read in their newfound passion or the repeated reading that is woven into the experience—they were able to overcome their reading difficulties by joining the school drama club and engaging in the repeated readings that were precursors to a performance for an audience. Finally, singing—whether in music class, the school glee club, or just in a classroom holiday performance, as long as it requires reading the lyrics—offers wonderful opportunities to engage in both wide and repeated reading with an emphasis on expressiveness. Poetry, too, can easily find its way into an extracurricular poetry club that meets and performs regularly outside of school.

But if you are a teacher, the venue you have the most control over is your classroom. We urge you to look for the 15 minutes a day to incorporate different reading strategies into your classroom. These 15 minutes could have a tremendous impact of your students' reading development.

MATERIALS

Fluency instruction requires you to think about texts in different ways. For traditional reading instruction, we often think of stories and informational texts. These can be rather lengthy texts that need to be read once over the course of several days or weeks. But, because fluency development requires a certain amount of assisted and repeated reading, the texts used for it cannot be excessively long. We feel that texts of one to three pages in length are ideal for fluency practice. Moreover, because prosody, or expressiveness, in oral reading is an essential component of fluency, the texts that are chosen for fluency should lend themselves to expressive, or prosodic, reading. As we have mentioned throughout this book, texts such as Readers Theatre scripts, poems, songs, monologues, dialogues, speeches, and the like are ideal texts for fluency instruction and development.

Published collections of scripts, poems, song lyrics, and other fluency texts are available from many educational publishers. These materials can also be found rather easily by searching the Internet. In Appendixes B through E we provide a listing of some of our favorite websites for engaging materials that can be used to develop reading fluency.

But you can also think beyond these text types. Often, stories have a strong voice that can easily be translated into an oral reading performance. The key here would be to find relatively short segments of longer stories that can be used for fluency practice. A multiple-paragraph segment can easily be found in most chapter books that students enjoy reading and performing for fluency. Comic books and graphic novels, by their very nature of conversation and thought balloons, can also be easily adapted for fluency development. One teacher we know keeps joke books around to build prosody, reasoning that in order for a joke to be told effectively, it has to be delivered in a certain way. And the only way to do that is to read it over and over until you get it right.

We mentioned in Chapter 6 the power of using phrasing to build fluency. Patterned and predictable books such as *Brown Bear, Brown Bear, What Do You See?* by Erik Carle are ideal for helping emerging readers to read in phrases. Other award-winning books with predicable text, such as *These Hands* by Margaret H. Mason and Floyd Cooper, are ideal for the upper grades and have the additional benefit of addressing age-appropriate content-area material. A list of notable predictable texts/books is offered in Appendix C.

The ultimate source for fluency materials, we feel, is you and your students. Through the process of repeated reading of scripts, poems, and other materials, you and your students will develop a good sense of the nature of the materials themselves. If you and your students are committed to fluency through a practice and performance model, it won't be long before you and your students are writing your own poems, songs, and other texts that can be modeled after the texts you have been performing. Students absolutely love writing and then practicing and performing their own version of Judith Viorst's *If I Were in Charge of the World* or *Yankee Doodle*. Bruce Lansky's website gigglepoetry.com actually provides lessons on how students can write their own versions of familiar rhymes. More and more teachers and students are making their own Readers Theatre scripts by adapting picture books, segments of chapter books, or even informational texts.

Some teachers have integrated fluency text writing with writing instruction by guiding students in creating their own scripts. We are sometimes asked if script writing is an authentic form of writing and writing instruction. All we have to do is go to Hollywood where we will find a whole community of writers who turn stories into scripts for television and movies. Indeed, we feel that turning a story into a script requires a fair amount of close or deep reading, as the script writer has to have an insightful understanding of the original text.

If you are interested in developing your own script, we suggest that you start with a short picture book that contains plenty of dialogue. The dialogue can easily be put into script form. You or your students should feel free to add narration, dialogue, and even characters to enhance the script. Once the script is developed, it can be added to your ever-growing compendium of fluency materials for future classes of students.

LESSON FORMAT COMPONENTS

Once you have set your fluency goals for your students, allotted time for fluency, and found and developed fluency materials, you need to consider how you will develop your instruction. Whether you put into place an existing lesson format, such as the Fluency Development Lesson, or develop your own instructional fluency routine, certain principles of fluency instruction should guide you. These are modeling, repetition and support, and performance. In a sense, these principles are a form of the guided release of responsibility that should be a common characteristic of nearly all forms of successful instruction.

I Do: Modeling

Students need to hear what fluent reading sounds like. Have them follow along as you read a short passage at an appropriate pace with good expression. Ask them to listen to you vary your pace and use your voice to tell the story. Then, as a contrast, with the same passage, model exaggerated or unexpressive reading. Ask them which they prefer and why. Whenever you, as the teacher, read aloud to students, do so with the energy and expression appropriate to the text. After reading a text to the students, discuss with them not only the content of the text but also what you did to make the reading more engaging and meaningful for the students. Of course, the message to students should be that they should try to incorporate the same features—both silently and aloud—in their own reading.

Models of fluent reading can also be found online at YouTube and similar sites. Simply search for *oral reading, poetry reading, Readers Theatre*, and similar terms. You and your students will find many examples of students and adults reading fluently (and sometimes not so fluently). These readings can be used as a way of discussing fluent and disfluent reading without embarrassing the students in your own class.

We Do: Repetition (Rehearsal) and Support

Repetition and support are the heart and soul of fluency development. Repeated reading with support will lead students from less-than-fluent reading to expressive, meaningful, and even joyful reading. The trick is in how you get it done without leading students to boredom. Keep it engaging, varied, and fun, and the students will think of it as play. If the students suspect drudgery, you may get no less in return. The essential goal of repeated reading is for students to practice a text until they achieve fluency. Repeated readings are best utilized with texts that have a strong sense of voice and that lend themselves to oral and expressive performance. As we mentioned earlier, such texts include scripts, poetry, song lyrics, speeches, cheers, chants, letters, and dialogues. Many texts, such as sing-alongs and choral and antiphonal readings can be whole-class, teacher-directed activities. Others, such as Readers Theatre, speeches, individual and shared poetry, and graphic novel creations, lend themselves to a performance venue in which smaller groups of students rehearse over a period of several days before performing.

You can offer support for your students by asking them to read a text while listening as either you or another fluent reader reads with them. Ask your students to read with you after you first model it, encouraging them to keep up with you. This is especially important when students read aloud chorally. There is a tendency for students to slow down to the rate of the slowest reader or slower. Anyone who has heard the "Happy Birthday Dirge" (see YouTube) can attest to this.

You Do: Performance

Performance of a text is the intrinsic motivator for rehearsal or repeated reading. It doesn't have to be a full-blown production. It can be anything from reading a rehearsed piece in front of a classmate, teacher, or parent to appearing before a schoolwide assembly. Figure 8.1 provides a quick outline of the considerations you need to make in developing performance-based fluency instruction. Granted, your students might initially be cautious about the prospect of performing. It has been our experience that with a little encouragement, when most get their feet wet, they decide that they enjoy the water.

A key to performance is setting the stage. You need to know when you want to have your performances: daily, at the end of each day; on Friday afternoons; or perhaps you'll take a special "fluency break" at surprise times throughout the day. Then, you'll need to consider who will perform and if you will need to spread students' performances over the course of several days.

Also, it is important to consider *where* you will be performing—in your classroom, another teacher's classroom, Carnegie Hall (We should be so lucky!), or the lunchroom. Maybe your school library has a special area for performing. Perhaps you can make your performers into a traveling road show as they go from one classroom to another to perform.

Some of your students may not be excited about performing right off. In fact, for reasons we stated earlier, they may be embarrassed to read in front of others. We recommend easing those students into performance. One way to do this is to create an offstage character

Figure 8.1. Fluency Development Framework

Step 1: Choose material

Instructional level
High interest
Suitable to oral reading

Step 2: Rehearse

Introduce text
Model
Practice
Vary assignments

Step 3: Perform

Establish venue
Invite audience
Celebrate

in a Readers Theatre script who delivers lines out of sight of the audience. For example, one teacher we know uses something he calls the Invisible Poet. He took a discarded cardboard refrigerator box and turned it into a makeshift radio booth. The students perform a script from behind a thin curtain and "broadcast" it as if on radio to the rest of the class. He had so much success with this that he recorded the performances and put them on the class website as podcasts called *The Room 103 Radio Hour*.

We offer one important caveat when it comes to performing. After having rehearsed a text several times, students may have it memorized and may want to perform it "by heart." Although you may allow your students to do that occasionally, remember that the goal of the performance is to develop reading fluency. Thus, we generally prefer that students have a copy of the texts they are reading in front of them and that they actually read the text while performing. Additionally, actually having a text to read will reduce much of the anxiety that many students may have when they are asked to perform.

In all performance situations, stress volume. Most commonly, we find that people listening to students perform say they have trouble hearing what is said. So, especially when performing in a place other than a small classroom, volume is of the utmost importance. One obvious way to achieve good volume to ensure that the scripts are not held in front of the students' faces. Another is to have the performers at one end of the classroom practice reading to students at the other end of the classroom. Ask particularly quiet readers to exaggerate. Tell them to imagine that you, the teacher, are extremely hard of hearing, and that in order for you to understand them, they must speak loudly and clearly.

Performance, of course, can take a variety of forms. In addition to performing before a large audience, students can perform for a parent or a volunteer, who may be sitting in the hallway outside the classroom. Tim often suggests that kids practice at home reading to their dog if they have one, because it's hard to find a better listener than man's best friend. Performances can also take the form of recording students' performances for the classroom website, for your ever-increasing collection of audio-recorded texts for your fluency center, or for the students' reading portfolio. By increasing the range of performance your students will be doing, you will also be increasing the level of interest and engagement for students.

FLUENCY INSTRUCTION IN ACTION

We would like to walk you through a possible instructional fluency scenario. In general, the lesson should start with the introduction of the chosen text, followed by modeling, student practice, and finally performance. All students should have access to the text. Be sure to make necessary accommodations for students who have visual perception issues. The introduction should include a brief explanation of what you are going to do and a quick familiarization of the text.

Next, model fluent expressive reading of the text, particularly parts that may be more complicated. Demonstrate how using good prosody can bring a script to life. Then, guide and support students in their first readings. This may be done in the form of choral reading, where the students read with you at an appropriate pace, or in echo reading, where the students repeat each phrase or sentence you read. Depending on the activity, students may break into small groups for individualized practice.

When speeches or poetry are being used, students may work in pairs, where both students can either whisper-read for familiarization or read aloud to their partners. When using Readers Theatre, consider a fishbowl demonstration of how to run a rehearsal. Assign each Readers Theatre group someone who will be called the show starter. In small-group rehearsal, the show starter initiates the reading. The roll rotates on a daily basis.

When working toward a presentation, you'll need to consider who, what, when, and where—who the audience will be, what will be performed, and when and where the presentation will take place.

Who

Who, of course, is for whom you will be performing—such as parents, peers, or other classes. Consider inviting parents to attend. The presence of the principal or vice principal also makes the performance a special event. If these individuals cannot come to your classroom, you may want to take the show on the road, so to speak, and visit other classrooms. This can be particularly effective when performing for classes in the lower grades. Besides building fluency in your students, an additional benefit of having, say, 5th-graders perform for 2nd-graders is the inspiration and modeling it provides for the younger students.

What

This is your choice of material. You'll want to choose something that is at the class's overall instructional level. The more challenging the material, the more time and support the students will need. You can tailor the parts to individuals' strengths, needs, and dispositions. You may start by casting to type—that is, the shy boy will play the part of a shy boy, a confident girl will play the part of a confident girl, and so forth. In the rehearsal process, always offer options for the students to read other parts. As they get more comfortable with the format, try casting against type. Challenge the boisterous boy to read the part of a timid character. Allow the student who may be socially awkward to be the star. By offering such options, you keep interest high and fluency development strong. In order to maintain the novelty, choose materials to perform that can be mastered in four or five 15-minute practice periods.

When

This is the time and day you will be performing—show time. We suggest developing a weekly routine. In the classroom, we find Friday afternoons work well because it offers a way to culminate a week of rehearsal, but you may find another time that fits better into your schedule. For bigger performances that take place outside the classroom, you might want to work backward on the calendar to ensure that the students are prepared for the event. We suggest that up until the last three read throughs, you vary the rehearsal activities, such as reading parts other than one's own and practicing alternate vocal interpretations, so the students stay "fresh" with their parts. The excitement of having a performance 2 or 3 days away usually brings out the best in students.

Where

You'll want to choose the place for your performance carefully. Your own classroom is usually the first and best choice, particularly for inexperienced performers, who will feel more comfortable in a familiar environment. As your students build confidence, consider larger venues such as the cafeteria or the school auditorium if your school has one. In all instances, keeping distractions to a minimum ensures a better experience for both students and audience.

Post-Performance

Take a minute to congratulate your performers, no matter the size of the venue. Be sure to invite the audience to show their appreciation as well. Allow your students to bask in the glow of a job well done. We can't think of a more natural and powerful motivation for the next round of fluency instruction. Once the students have performed, you might have the student audience offer their own oral response to the performance or ask audience members to fill out a peer performance rubric (Figure 8.2). The performers also may fill out a fluency self-assessment (Figure 8.3). Get them to pay special attention to the *What I might do differently next time* section.

PROGRESS MONITORING

You will want to know if the fluency instruction you are completing with your students is having the desired effect. Be sure to plan regular times to monitor your students' progress. Once every 4 to 6 weeks should be sufficient. The 3-Minute Reading Assessment (3MRA) is a simple, quick, and efficient way to monitor fluency progress as well as progress in other areas of reading. Compare your students' individual performance over time. If your instruction is working, you should be seeing growth in most areas of reading from one administration to the next.

BENEFITS OF FLUENCY INSTRUCTION

The purpose of fluency instruction is to ensure that students' growth in reading and content-knowledge acquisition is not impeded by a lack of fluency. The primary goal is to improve fluency so it can lead to growth in reading comprehension and overall learning. A growing and compelling body of research supports the use of fluency instruction across the grade levels to increase student reading engagement, student self-confidence as readers and learners, and especially comprehension of texts read both silently and orally.

Fluency development is critical to developing a solid foundation for all reading. The foundational competencies (K–5) of the Common

Figure 8.2. Peer Performance Fluency Assessment

Performer(s) _____

	3	2	1
Expression	Overall expression was excellent.	Expression was sometimes pretty good.	There wasn't much expression in the reading.
Pace and Timing	There were very few awkward pauses. The pace and timing made it believable.	There were some awkward pauses, but . . .	There were a lot of awkward pauses.
Volume and Clarity	All lines could be heard and understood.	Some lines could not be heard and understood.	Most lines could not be heard or understood.
Overall enjoyment	I loved it!	It was okay.	Not really my cup of tea.

Figure 8.3. Fluency Self-Assessment

Name _____

	3	2	1
Expression	I read with excellent expression.	I read sometimes with good expression.	My expression wasn't so good today.
Timing	My timing was almost perfect.	My timing was a little off today.	My timing was way off today.
Volume	I read with good volume.	My volume was sometimes too low.	I muttered most of my lines.
What I might do differently next time:			

Core State Standards (CCSS) note that proficient readers need to read a level of word recognition accuracy and fluency that leads to comprehension. Without sufficient fluency, comprehension will be hampered, and the students will not have mastered the standards for their grade level(s).

One of the College and Career Readiness Anchor Standards for Reading in the CCSS states that students should be able to "read closely to determine what the text says explicitly and to make logical inferences from it" (National Governors Association Center for Best Practices & Council of Chief State School Officers, 2010, p.11). Recent research suggests that many fluency exercises, particularly those involving the rehearsal and performance of scripts and other texts, contribute to the development of close reading and inferencing skills (Nageldinger, 2014). In order to master a text to the point of performing it with meaning and expression, the student has to engage in multiple readings and focusing on various features of the text with each reading. Fluency activities that involve oral interpretation, such as speeches, poems, and Readers Theatre scripts, are particularly well positioned to address the close reading standard.

MRS. RADOVITCH REVISITED

Recall that in Chapter 3, Mrs. Radovitch had just given five of her students the 3-Minute Reading Assessment and found that they were in need of fluency development. We caught up with her 7 months later for an update.

First, she told us that the 3-Minute Reading Assessment gave her insight into which students were struggling with which particular aspects of fluency. After the assessment, she started to set aside 15 minutes a day for fluency development. The first thing she tried was repeated choral reading of texts from the social studies textbook. She said that the students did it, but were not particularly engaged. She said:

> So I shifted gears. I took part of our instructional time and explained about how characters in movies and on TV shows did what they did by explaining the idea of scripts. I held up a script and I told them that to get started all actors read their lines to each other. We were going to do the same. I took your advice and started with something simple.

She found a script developed from *Frog and Toad Are Friends*, "Spring," by Arnold Lobel. It was written for four parts, but she was able to create a fifth part by borrowing some on the narrator's lines and giving them to the new part. Before she handed out a script, she explained what was happening in the script and who the characters were. She pretaught and modeled some of the new words and told students to pay attention to how she pronounced them in the scripts.

> I projected the script using my document camera and we had a shared reading. Actually, it was an echo read—I read a line, then they repeated it. I did my best to read with good expression. Then, we did a read through together. I did this so that they could get a sense of the ideal pace.

She said the scripts she handed out all had a different part highlighted so it was easier for them to identify which lines they should read out loud. To make things clear and simple, she highlighted each script with a different color. In this case, Frog's script had his lines highlighted in green, Toad's were in yellow, Narrator 1's were in pink, and so on. Now it was time to get under way.

> To get started, I took your advice and told them that I would cue the first line by making eye contact with the first reader and nodding my head. And, we were off. The first reading was a bit shaky—there were a number of missed cues and some stumbling on new words. So after the first read through, I asked them to practice whisper-reading just their lines until they felt they could say them well. During this time, I circulated and listened, offering support, advice, and modeling when needed. Then we all came together again for another reading. The second read through went much better. It was a great way to end our first fluency development session.

The next day, she did more of the same with her students until they were all comfortable with their parts. Then she asked another teacher to come in and listen for a few minutes. She said, "They were so proud of their performance! As a teacher, seeing pride in the eyes of kids who don't get a lot of strokes for things they do in school was so satisfying."

After that first successful run-through, she told students they could choose a different part to read. She solved the problem of more than one person wanting to read a particular part by ensuring them that everybody would get a chance to read any part that he or she wanted: "By the end of the week, I estimated every one of my five students had read the script no less than 15 times, without even one complaint!"

She told us from then on it became a part of her weekly routine. Every Monday, she would "book talk" two or three new scripts and ask which ones sounded interesting to the students. Unanimous choices were used that week, and the others were put away for another time. The class would practice the next couple of days and on Friday have a short performance. As students' confidence and fluency increased, she offered more-challenging scripts, being sure to include the kind she knew they would find interesting.

> Long story short, for the most part they have been having a ball with this. But more importantly, they are sounding like real readers now, and when I gave the 3-Minute Reading Assessment last month, they all showed growth that is approaching or at grade-level expectations. I couldn't be more pleased!

CLOSING COMMENTS

Now it is up to you. We hope you are now ready to jump into fluency instruction, or if you are already implementing fluency instruction with your students, that you may want to alter your instruction based on what you have read.

Reading achievement in the United States has largely remained stagnant over the past 20-plus years. We can't help but wonder if one reason for this stagnation is that fluency continues to be neglected (Allington, 1983), misunderstood, and viewed as not important for reading success. We feel that fluency instruction, done in an engaging, scientific, and artful manner, may just be the ticket for increasing reading achievement in students, especially for those students who find reading difficult. We wish you and your students happy and fluent reading!

A Compendium of Fluency Building Activities

Throughout this book we have introduced you to a number activities that have been shown to increase reading fluency. Below is a listing of instructional activities that lend themselves to the development of reading fluency while keeping students engaged. We encourage you to keep this list handy and commit to using at least one of the activities each week.

- *Antiphonal Reading:* In this fluency building activity, also sometimes called call and response, the teacher chooses short sentences that are sung or recited, alternating between two or more groups of readers. Instead of one person calling and a group responding, antiphonal reading divides students into roughly equal groups. One group leads off reading the first line in unison and the next group responds reading the second line in unison. Poetry lends itself especially well to antiphonal reading. Groups should be flexible and can be determined by gender, sides of the classroom, birthday months, and so on.
- *Audio-Assisted Reading:* Student listens to a recorded reading of a book or play while simultaneously following along in the actual text. This activity has proven especially effective with middle and upper grades reading Shakespeare. As little as 15 minutes a day can have a great impact.
- *Choral Reading:* In this fluency building activity, everyone reads the same passage aloud in one voice. It is important that the teacher or another expert reader model the reading first and set the tone and pace. This activity is often used as an introduction to antiphonal reading.
- *Chants, Cheers, Handclaps:* Students use traditional chants, cheers, and handclaps. This works best with text with repeating words or

patterns such as Miss Mary Mack. The students agree on simple hand gestures to go with certain words, such as a clap, wave, or a circular motion. Then one student reads as the other performs the assigned actions. Students later switch roles. This works well with younger readers.

- **Dialogues—Spoken Comics:** This activity works well with students who like to read comic books. In this activity the student chooses a character from a comic book or graphic novel. A parent, teacher, or other students read aloud with the student using appropriate expression. Encourage the student to use different voices. Switch parts and find someone to perform for.

- **Paired Reading:** The student selects a text, and then either a parent, a teacher, or another student reads aloud with him or her. This allows a struggling reader to hear good reading at an appropriate pace. Depending on the student's needs, the "helper" either slightly leads or follows the student. Eventually the student will progress to reading alone.

- **Poetry in Pairs:** In this form of paired reading, the student selects a poem for two voices, and then a parent, a teacher, or other student reads aloud with him or her. After several readings, the student and other reader switch parts.

- **Readers Theatre:** This powerful fluency building activity is a form of theatre in which there is minimal movement and few props or costumes, and it is excellent for improving expressive reading, since the meaning of the play is determined by the voice-along. Participating students stand in a line and read their assigned characters' lines from a play script written for oral performance. The students practice for a few minutes each day, leading to a performance at the end of the week.

- **Singing:** Students are given a text to follow, along with recorded music. Choose blues, jazz, rock, folk songs, or show tunes with rich music and interesting lyrics. While the music plays, students keep track of the words as they sing the lyrics. To ensure your students are reading rather than reciting, change songs frequently and provide a varied repertoire.

- **Speeches:** Speeches are rehearsed with elocution and oral interpretation in mind. This is a great way to increase fluency while teaching social studies.

Poetry Sources

Online Resources

www.brodbagert.com
www.gigglepoetry.com
www.jackprelutsky.com
www.poets.org/poetsorg/materials-teachers
www.poetrysoup.com/poems/best/middle_school
www.poetryfoundation.org/downloads/BHM_MiddleSchool.pdf
www.poetry4kids.com
www.rainydaypoems.com/poems-for-kids
www.robertpottle.com
www.saraholbrook.com
www.writersdigest.com/whats-new/poems-for-kids

Books of Poetry

Brod Bagert, *Giant Children*, 2005, New York, NY: Puffin.
Paul Fleischman, *Joyful Noise: Poems for Two Voices*, 2004, New York, NY: Harper Collins.
Sara Holbrook, *The Dog Ate My Homework*, 1996, New York, NY: Scholastic.
Bruce Lansky, *If Pigs Could Fly*, 2000, Minnetonka, MN: Meadowbrook.
Shel Silverstein, *Where the Sidewalk Ends*, 2014, New York, NY: Harper Collins.

Patterned and Predictable Texts

By Title

A Fine, Fine School	Creech, S. (2001)	New York, NY: HarperCollins
Boston Tea Party	Edwards, P. (2001)	New York, NY: G.P. Putnam's Sons
Brown Bear, Brown Bear, What Do You See?	Carle, E. (1996)	New York, NY: Henry Holt and Co.
Butterflies Fly	Winer, Y. (2001)	Watertown, MA: Charlesbridge
Dolores Huerta, a Hero to Migrant Workers	Warren, S. (2012)	Tarrytown, NY: Marshall Cavendish Corporation
Fortunately	Charlip, R. (1993)	New York, NY: Trumpet Club
Full House: An Invitation to Fractions	Dodds, D. A., & Carter, A. (2009)	Somerville, MA: Candlewick
Gotta Go! Gotta Go!	Swope, S., & Riddle, S. (2004)	New York, NY: Square Fish, Macmillan
These Hands	Mason, M. H. (2011)	New York, NY: HMH Books for Young Readers
This Is the Rope: A Story from the Great Migration	Woodson, J. (2013)	New York, NY: Nancy Paulsen Books

By Author

Carle, E. (1996)	*Brown Bear, Brown Bear, What Do You See?*	New York, NY: Henry Holt and Co.
Charlip, R. (1993)	*Fortunately*	New York, NY: Trumpet Club.
Creech, R. (1993)	*A Fine, Fine School*	New York, NY: Harper Collins
Dodds, D. A., & Carter, A. (2009)	*Full House: An Invitation to Fractions*	Somerville, MA: Candlewick
Edwards, P. (2001)	*Boston Tea Party*	New York, NY: G. P. Putnam's Sons
Mason, M. H. (2011)	*These Hands*	New York, NY: HMH Books for Young Readers
Swope, S., & Riddle, S. (2004	*Gotta Go! Gotta Go!*	New York, NY: Square Fish, Macmillan
Warren, S. (2012)	*Dolores Huerta, a Hero to Migrant Workers*	Tarrytown, NY: Marshall Cavendish Corporation
Winer, Y. (2001)	*Butterflies Fly*	Watertown, MA: Charlesbridge
Woodson, J. (2013)	*This Is the Rope: A Story from the Great Migration*	New York, NY: Nancy Paulsen Books

Website Sources for Readers Theatre Scripts and Information About Readers Theatre

www.aaronshep.com/rt
www.fictionteachers.com/classroomtheater/theater.html
www.busyteacherscafe.com/literacy/readers_theater.html
rtscripts.weebly.com/index.html
www.superteacherworksheets.com/readers-theater.html
www.teachingheart.net/readerstheater.htm
www.thebestclass.org/rtscripts.html
www.timelessteacherstuff.com
www.timrasinski.com
www.vtaide.com/png/theatre.htm

Website and Article Sources for Singing in the Classroom

www.contemplator.com/america
www.niehs.nih.gov/kids/music.htm
www.scoutsongs.com/categories/patriotic-songs.html
www.songsforteaching.com
www.theteachersguide.com/ChildrensSongs.htm

Resources for more information on using handclap songs, chants, cadences, and marching songs to promote literacy across the curriculum

Batchelor, K. E., & Bintz, W. P. (2012). Hand-clap songs across the curriculum. *The Reading Teacher, 65*(5), 341–344.

Ciecierski, L., & Bintz, W. P. (2012). Using chants and cadences to promote literacy across the curriculum. *Middle School Journal (J3), 44*(2), 22–29.

Nageldinger, J. K., & Bintz, W. P. (2012). Marching songs across the curriculum. *Language Experience Forum Journal, 42*(2), 4–14.

References

Allington, R. L. (1983). Fluency: The neglected reading goal. *The Reading Teacher, 36,* 556–561.

Allington, R. L., McGill-Franzen, A., Camilli, G., Williams, L., Graff, J., Zeig, J., Zmach, C., & Nowak, R. (2010). Addressing summer reading setback among economically disadvantaged elementary students. *Reading Psychology, 31*(5), 411–427.

Beaver, J., Carter, M., Sreenivasan, J., Leon, V., & Siburt, R. (2004). *Developmental reading assessment.* New York, NY: Pearson Educational.

Biggs, M. C., Homan, S. P., Dedrick, R., Minick, V., & Rasinski, T. (2008). Using an interactive singing software program: A comparative study of struggling middle school readers. *Reading Psychology, 29*(3), 195–213. doi:10.1080/02702710802073438

Bushnell, R., Miller, A., & Robson, D. (1982). Parents as remedial teachers: An account of a paired-reading project with junior school failing readers and their parents. *AEP (Association of Educational Psychologists) Journal, 5*(9), 7–13.

Carroll, L. (1897). *Through the looking-glass, and what Alice found there.* Philadelphia, PA: Henry Altemus.

Chall, J. S. (1996). *Stages of reading development* (2nd ed.). Fort Worth, TX: Harcourt-Brace.

Chomsky, C. (1976). After decoding: What? *Language Arts, 53,* 288–296.

Clay, M. (2000). *Running records for teachers.* Portsmouth, NH: Heinemann.

Crosby, S. A., Rasinski, T., Padak, N., & Yildirim, K. (2014). A 3-year study of a school-based parental involvement program in early literacy. *Journal of Educational Research, 108,* 165–172.

Daane, M. C., Campbell, J. R., Grigg, W. S., Goodman, M. J., & Oranje, A. (2005). *Fourth-grade students reading aloud: NAEP 2002 special study of oral reading.* Washington, DC: U.S. Department of Education, Institute of Education Sciences.

Durkin, D. (1966). *Children who read early: Two longitudinal studies.* New York, NY: Teachers College Press.

Eldredge, J. L., & Butterfield, D. D. (1986). Alternatives to traditional reading instruction. *The Reading Teacher, 40,* 32–37.

Eldredge, J. L., & Quinn, W. (1988). Increasing reading performance of low-achieving second graders by using dyad reading groups. *Journal of Educational Research, 82*, 40–46.

Fuchs, L. S., Fuchs, D., Hosp, M. K., & Jenkins, J. R. (2001). Oral reading fluency as an indicator of reading competence: A theoretical, empirical, and historical analysis. *Scientific Studies of Reading, 5*(3), 239–256.

Goodman, Y., Watson, D., & Burke, C. (2005). *Reading miscue inventory.* Katonah, NY: Richard C. Owen.

Heckelman, R. G. (1969). A neurological impress method of reading instruction. *Academic Therapy, 4*, 277–282.

Herman, P. A. (1985). The effect of repeated readings on reading rate, speech pauses, and word recognition accuracy. *Reading Research Quarterly, 20*(5), 553–565.

Hoffman, J. V., & Segel, K. (1983, May). Oral reading instruction: A century of controversy (1880–1980). Paper presented at the annual meeting of the International Reading Association, Anaheim, CA. (ERIC Document Reproduction Service No. ED239237).

Huey, E. B. (1908). *The psychology and pedagogy of reading.* Boston, MA: MIT Press.

Hyatt, A. V. (1943). *The place of oral reading in the school program: Its history and development from 1880–1941.* New York, NY: Teachers College, Columbia University.

James, W. (1892). *Psychology.* New York, NY: Holt.

Jenkins, J. R., Fuchs, L. S., van den Broek, P., Espin, C., & Deno, S. L. (2003). Sources of individual differences in reading comprehension and reading fluency. *Journal of Educational Psychology, 95*(4), 719–729. doi:10.1037/0022-0663.95.4.719

Kuhn, M. R., Schwanenflugel, P. J., Meisinger, E. B., Levy, B. A., & Rasinski, T. V. (2010). Aligning theory and assessment of reading fluency: Automaticity, prosody, and definitions of fluency. *Reading Research Quarterly, 45*(2), 230–251.

LaBerge, D., & Samuels, S. J. (1974). Toward a theory of automatic information processing in reading. *Cognitive Psychology, 6*, 293–323.

Leslie, L., & Caldwell, J. A. (2011). *Qualitative reading inventory: 5.* Boston, MA: Pearson/Allyn & Bacon.

Lewis, T. E. (2012). *The aesthetics of education: Theatre, curiosity, and politics in the work of Jacques Ranciere and Paolo Freire.* New York, NY: Continuum International.

Limbrick, L., McNaughton, S., & Cameron, M. (1985). *Peer tutoring: Update.* Birmingham, UK: Positive Products.

Miller, J., & Schwanenflugel, P. J. (2008). A longitudinal study of the development of reading prosody as a dimension of oral reading fluency in early elementary school children. *Reading Research Quarterly, 43*(4), 336–354.

Morgan, D., Mraz, M., Padak, N., & Rasinski, T. (2008). *Independent reading.* New York, NY: Guilford.

Nageldinger, J. (2014). *An investigation into the impact of theatre and drama activities on struggling readers* (Unpublished doctoral dissertation). Kent State University, Kent, OH.

National Reading Panel. (2000). *Report of the National Reading Panel: Teaching children to read. Report of the subgroups.* Washington, DC: U.S. Department of Health and Human Services, National Institutes of Health.

National Governors Association Center for Best Practices & Council of Chief State School Officers. (2010). *Common Core State Standards.* Retrieved from www.corestandards.org

Padak, N., & Rasinski, T. (2004). Fast Start: A promising practice for family literacy programs. *Family Literacy Forum, 3,* 3–9.

Paige, D. D. (2011). "That sounded good!" Using whole-class choral reading to improve fluency. *The Reading Teacher, 64,* 435–438.

Paige, D. D. (in press). 16 minutes with eyes of text can make a difference: Whole-class choral reading as a fluency strategy. *Reading Horizons.*

Paige, D. D., Rasinski, T. V., & Magpuri-Lavell, T. (2012). Is fluent, expressive reading important for high school readers? *Journal of Adolescent & Adult Literacy, 56*(1), 67–76.

Parker, F. W. (1894). *Talks on pedagogics.* New York, NY: Barnes and Co.

Pikulski, J. J., & Chard, D. J. (2005). Fluency: Bridge between decoding and reading comprehension. *The Reading Teacher, 58*(6), 510–519.

Pinnell, G. S., Pikulski, J. J., Wixson, K. K., Campbell, J. R., Gough, P. B., & Beatty, A. S. (1995). *Listening to children read aloud.* Washington, DC: U.S. Department of Education, Office of Educational Research and Improvement.

Postlethwaite, T. N., & Ross, K. N. (1992). *Effective schools in reading: Implications for policy planner.* The Hague, Netherlands: International Association for the Evaluation of Educational Achievement.

Rasinski, T. V. (1995). Fast Start: A parental involvement reading program for primary grade students. In W. Linek & E. Sturtevant (Eds.), *Generations of literacy. Seventeenth yearbook of the College Reading Association* (pp. 301–312). Harrisonburg, VA: College Reading Association.

Rasinski, T. V. (2010). *The fluent reader: Oral and silent reading strategies for building word recognition, fluency, and comprehension* (2nd ed.). New York, NY: Scholastic.

Rasinski, T. V. (2011). The art and science of teaching reading fluency. In D. Lapp, N. Frey, & D. Fisher (Eds.), *Handbook of Research on Teaching the English Language Arts* (3rd ed., pp. 238–246). New York, NY: Routledge.

Rasinski, T., & Hamman, P. (2010). Fluency: Why it is "not hot." *Reading Today, 28,* 26.

Rasinski, T. V., & Hoffman, J. V. (2003). Theory and research into practice: Oral reading in the school literacy curriculum. *Reading Research Quarterly, 38,* 510–522.

Rasinski, T. V., & Padak, N. (2005a). 3-minute reading assessments: Word recognition, fluency, and comprehension, grades 1–4. New York, NY: Scholastic.

Rasinski, T. V., & Padak, N. (2005a). 3-minute reading assessments: Word recognition, fluency, and comprehension, grades 5–8. New York, NY: Scholastic.

Rasinski, T. V., & Padak, N. D. (2005b). Fluency beyond the primary grades: Helping adolescent readers. *Voices from the Middle, 13,* 34–41.

Rasinski, T. V., Padak, N., & Fawcett, G. (2009). *Teaching children who find reading difficult* (4th ed.). New York, NY: Pearson.

Rasinski, T. V., Padak, N. D., Linek, W. L., & Sturtevant, E. (1994). Effects of fluency development on urban second-grade readers. *Journal of Educational Research, 87,* 158–165.

Rasinski, T., Padak, N., McKeon, C., Krug-Wilfong, L., Friedauer, J., & Heim, P. (2005). Is reading fluency a key for successful high school reading? *Journal of Adolescent and Adult Literacy, 49,* 22–27.

Rasinski, T. V., Reutzel, D. R., Chard, D., & Linan-Thompson, S. (2011). Reading fluency. In M. L. Kamil, P. D. Pearson, B. Moje, & P. Afflerbach (Eds.), *Handbook of reading research* (Vol. iv, pp. 286–319). New York, NY: Routledge.

Rasinski, T., Riki, A., & Johnston, S. (2009). Reading fluency: More than automaticity? More than a concern for the primary grades? *Literacy Research and Instruction, 48,* 350–361.

Rasinski, T., & Stevenson, B. (2005). The effects of Fast Start reading, A fluency based home involvement reading program, on the reading achievement of beginning readers. *Reading Psychology: An International Quarterly, 26,* 109–125.

Reutzel, D. R., Jones, C., Fawson, P., & Smith, J. (2008). Scaffolded silent reading: A complement to guided repeated oral reading that works! *The Reading Teacher, 62,* 194–207. doi:10.1598/RT.62.3.2

Rose, D. S., Parks, M., Androes, K., & McMahon, S. D. (2001). Imagery-based learning: Improving elementary students' reading comprehension with drama techniques. *Journal of Educational Research, 94*(1), 55–63.

Samuels, S. J. (1979). The method of repeated readings. *The Reading Teacher, 32*(4), 403–408.

Samuels, S. J., Rasinski, T., & Hiebert, E. (2011). Eye movements and reading: What teachers need to know. In S. J. Samuels & A. E. Farstrup (Eds.), *What research has to say about reading instruction* (4th ed., pp. 25–50). Newark, DE: International Reading Association.

Scarborough, H. S. (2001). Connecting early language and literacy to later reading (dis)abilities: Evidence, theory, and practice. In S. B. Neuman & D. K. Dickinson (Eds.), *Handbook of early literacy research* (pp. 97–110). New York, NY: Guilford.

Schreiber, P. A. (1980). On the acquisition of reading fluency. *Journal of Reading Behavior, 12*, 177–186.

Schreiber, P. A. (1987). Prosody and structure in children's syntactic processing. In R. Horowitz & S. J. Samuels (Eds.), *Comprehending oral and written language* (pp. 243–270). New York, NY: Academic Press.

Schreiber, P. A. (1991). Understanding prosody's role in reading acquisition. *Theory into Practice, 30*, 158–164.

Schreiber, P. A., & Read, C. (1980). Children's use of phonetic cues in spelling, parsing, and—maybe—reading. *Bulletin of the Orton Society, 30*, 209–224.

Sénéchal, M. (2006). Testing the home literacy model: Parental involvement in kindergarten is differentially related to grade 4 reading comprehension, fluency, spelling, and reading for pleasure. *Scientific Studies in Reading, 10*, 59–87.

Sénéchal, M., & LeFevre, J. (2002). Parental involvement in the development of children's reading skill: A 5-year longitudinal study. *Child Development, 73*, 445–460.

Skinner, B. F. (1954). The science of learning and the art of teaching. *Harvard Educational Review, 24*(2), 86–97.

Smith, N. B. (1965). *American reading instruction.* Newark, DE: International Reading Association.

Stahl, S., & Heubach, K. (2005). Fluency-oriented reading instruction. *Journal of Literacy Research, 37*, 25–60.

Stanovich, K. E. (1986). Matthew effects in reading: Some consequences of individual differences in the acquisition of literacy. *Reading Research Quarterly, 21*, 360–407.

Steinhauer, K. (2003). Electrophysiological correlates of prosody and punctuation. *Brain and Language, 86*(1), 142–164. doi:10.1016/S0093-934X (02)00542-4

Thorndike, E. (1898). Some experiments on animal intelligence. *Science, 7*(181), 818–824. doi:10.1126/science.7.181.818

Topping, K. (1987a). Paired reading: A powerful technique for parent use. *The Reading Teacher, 40*, 604–614.

Topping, K. (1987b). Peer tutored paired reading: Outcome data from ten projects. *Educational Psychology, 7*, 133–145.

Topping, K. (1989). Peer tutoring and paired reading. Combining two powerful techniques. *The Reading Teacher, 42*, 488–494.

Trelease, J. (2006). *The read-aloud handbook* (6th ed.). New York, NY: Penguin.

Valencia, S. W., & Buly, M. R. (2004). Behind test scores: What struggling readers really need. *The Reading Teacher, 57*, 520–531.

Whitehurst, G. J., & Lonigan, C. J. (2001). Emergent literacy: Development from prereaders to readers. In S. B. Neuman & D. K. Dickinson (Eds.), *Handbook of early literacy research* (pp. 11–29). New York, NY: Guilford.

Wilks, R. T., & Clarke, V. A. (1988). Training versus nontraining of mothers as home reading tutors. *Perceptual and Motor Skills, 67,* 135–142.

Zimmerman, B. S., Rasinski, T. V., Kruse, S. D., Was, C., Dunlosky, J., & Rawson, K. (2012). *Enhancing outcomes for struggling readers: An empirical analysis of the Fluency Development Lesson.* Unpublished manuscript.

Zimmerman, B. S., Rasinski, T. V., & Melewski, M. (2013). When kids can't read, what a focus on fluency can do: The reading clinic experience at Kent State University. In E. Ortleib & E. Cheek (Eds.), *Advanced literacy practices: From the clinic to the classroom* (pp. 137–160). Bingley, England: Emerald Group.

Index

The letter *f* following a page number indicates a figure.

About the Authors

Timothy Rasinski has been engaged in practical and scholarly activity in literacy education since the late 1970s when he worked as an elementary school intervention reading teacher. His interest in fluency developed as he observed that a disproportionate number of students he worked with manifested difficulties in some aspect of reading fluency. His dissertation study on reading fluency at the Ohio State University in 1985 developed a theoretical model of reading that included reading fluency as a critical component. Since coming to Kent State University in 1988, where he is currently a professor of literacy education, Tim has continued to study reading fluency, especially as it impacts struggling readers. Tim's scholarly work has been published in major scholarly journals such as *The Reading Teacher, Reading Research Quarterly, Reading Psychology,* and the *Journal of Educational Research.* His scholarly contributions to the field of literacy education also include stints as an editor of *The Reading Teacher* and the *Journal of Literacy Research.* Tim served a 3-year term on the board of directors of the International Reading Association and is a sought-after speaker at professional conferences on literacy education. In 2010, Tim was inducted into the International Reading Hall of Fame.

James Nageldinger is an assistant professor at Elmira College in upstate New York, where he works as a teacher educator. An undergraduate degree in theatre arts first got him interested in the idea that expressive oral reading was related to silent reading comprehension. After earning a master's in special education from the University of Washington, he spent his early years in education working with struggling readers in a high-poverty remote part of the Big Island of Hawaii. James's increasing inquiry into reading fluency led him to Kent State University, where he pursued a doctorate in curriculum and instruction with an emphasis on literacy. His dissertation, under the direction of Drs. Timothy Rasinski and William Bintz, on the collateral impact of school theatre programs on struggling readers was singled out for the American Reading Forum's 2014 Outstanding Graduate Student Research Paper Award. In addition to several book chapters on various aspects of reading fluency, his scholarly work can be found in numerous publications including *The Reading Teacher, Language Experience Forum Journal,* and the *Journal of Educational Research.*

Printed and bound by CPI Group (UK) Ltd, Croydon, CR0 4YY

09/06/2025

14685933-0002